COURTENAY LLOYD ENJOYING
A GLASS OF VODKA
MADRID 2016.

THE
BIOGRAPHY OF
C. COURTENAY LLOYD

MASHA LLOYD

The Biography of C. Courtenay Lloyd

Published in Great Britain by

L.R. Price Publications Ltd, 2021

27 Old Gloucester Street,
London, WC1N 3AX
www.lrpricepublications.com

Cover artwork by Maria Lloyd

ISBN: 9781916467996

BIOGRAPHY OF
C. COURTENAY LLOYD

*Memories of my father and the unknown story
of the remarkable life of an Englishman,
told in the year of his centenary.*

*By his daughter
Masha Lloyd*

Be a good beast, suffer in silence (anonymous)

These were words on a picture of a fawn above his bed when he was a child. These words define the way my father would live his life.

A perfectly reliable boy (school teacher Clifton College, Bristol)

These are the final words on his school report when he left in 1935. The school teacher was right. That is what he has always been; a perfectly reliable boy, a perfectly reliable officer in the navy, a perfectly reliable husband, a perfectly reliable father and grandfather as well as a perfectly reliable teacher and a perfectly reliable man.

A WWII Royal Navy veteran officer who contributed to the Liberation of Norway; an intelligence officer in the Allied Control Commission in Germany; a graduate of Selwyn College, Cambridge and teacher of spies in the Cold War; an English gentleman who married a Russian princess; a teacher of Russian at the RAF College Cranwell and inspirational master of Modern Languages at Bradford Grammar School for nearly 20 years. An exceptional and extraordinary man who turned one hundred years old on 1 May 2019.

This book is the biography of his life written by his daughter Masha Lloyd in the year of his centenary 2019 which was also the 80th anniversary of the start of WWII. Her father is one of the few veterans still alive able to tell their story first-hand.

The author gives a bird's-eye view of her father's and mother's lives which were most unconventional for England during their times. Her mother was a penniless aristocratic Russian refugee when she met her future husband, a man of genteel English extraction, yet opposites attracted. Their household and style of life would reflect that contrast and Masha Lloyd's tales of their quirky, eccentric, extremely international and rather unorthodox style of living make for entertaining reading, as do the many colourful characters who entered their lives. This book is a serious biography but peppered throughout with the most fascinating and often very funny anecdotes of the lives of Courtenay, his family and ancestors spanning the last ten decades.

Charles Courtenay Lloyd is a much loved and exceptional teacher, lifelong linguist, and former WWII Royal Navy (RNVR) veteran officer who contributed to the liberation of Norway, spending a year and a half after the war with the British Admiralty helping the country back on its feet. He was awarded the Liberty Medal from King Haakon VII and on his centenary King Haakon VII's grandson, the current King of Norway, Harald V, sent him a signed birthday card in recognition for his services to Norway in WWII. For a further two years he served as an intelligence officer with the Control Commission in Germany, restoring order and helping dismantle the legacy of the Nazi regime which included catching war criminals on the run and helping with the establishment of a new political party.

Born on 1 May 1919 in Amington (County Warwick), he was the son of a clergyman, Revd Canon John Collins Lloyd, and Dorothy Gertrude Lloyd née Scull, an accomplished pianist.

He is an old Cliftonian (a former pupil of Clifton College, Bristol) who went on to graduate in German and Scandinavian languages from Selwyn College Cambridge and is the oldest living pupil of both educational establishments. During the cold war he was a teacher of spies with the Joint Services School for Linguists (JSSL) and later a teacher of Russian at RAF College Cranwell. From 1964 until his retirement in 1983 he was a senior master of Modern Languages at Bradford Grammar School, one of the best schools in the country. As a young man he married a Russian princess, Her Serene Highness Princess Elena von Lieven and they had two children, George and Masha.

He lost his wife to cancer in 1999 and his son George died two years later aged only 46. Earlier in life he lost his brother and sister both of whom also died at a tragically young age: Raymond who succumbed to polio in 1938 aged 16, and Gloria who was killed in an air crash aged 45 along with all her family in 1971. He is a person who has lost nearly everyone dear to him in life, including his own son. Yet he has always stoically soldiered on, conscientiously giving his all to everything he did and taking pleasure from the small things in life. This is something he taught his daughter and in this book her aim was to bring back to life, at least on the pages of this biography, all those close to him who he had lost so that they should never be forgotten.

In 2005 this remarkable man left Bradford and moved to Madrid. He has lived there ever since with his only surviving relatives, his daughter Masha, her husband Eladio and their two daughters Suzy and Olivia.

CONTENTS

This biography is an act of duty and of love. It is written on the occasion of my father turning one hundred on 1 May 2019 and for all the family we lost: his brother Raymond; his sister Gloria and his brother-in-law Derek along with their children, his little niece and nephews and my little cousins, Jacqueline, Michael and Anthony; Elena his wife and my mother; George, his son and my brother; Aunty Masha my mother's youngest sister and his closest sister-in-law. They all died too early in life and we carry them forever in our hearts. Only he and I remain today. On these pages I have brought them back to life as they can never be forgotten.

It is written in homage to my father, an extraordinary man who I have admired and respected always. It is also dedicated to all those who fell in WWII or who served valiantly and survived like him. It was time to tell the story of his contribution to the war. It is also dedicated to my own family, my steadfast and loving husband Eladio and to our children, Suzy and Olivia, for them to learn the true story of their grandfather and his family, their ancestors.

My father has lived with us since 2005 and it is only now that I have written his biography that I have really come to know the man who, although he has always been there for me, I never really knew and just took for granted. During our many slow conversations in the weeks it took to write his story, I finally got through his shyness and modesty, got closer to him and realized how much I love and admire him, and what a fascinating life he has led.

He is one of the few WWII veterans still alive. This book is also the story of his war and an appreciation of his contribution to the peace and unity they all achieved for us. They should always be remembered.

When I was young I was not interested in his stories of the war and didn't know who was who when he talked about Uncle Tom, Uncle Will, Aunty Nell, Aunty Gwen or Aunty Peggy, nor who his cousins were in Scotland. I didn't listen when he told me about some medal awarded to an Uncle David by the King of Siam, nor did I want to hear about his trips to Belgium, Finland, Switzerland, Germany, Iceland and Norway before and after the war. I thought his travel books published in the 1930s were not particularly useful. Now when I see his old Baedeker guidebooks, one of them in Swedish on Sweden and Norway printed in 1936, I am impressed. Now that I finally wanted to tell his story I only wished I had listened when I was younger.

The fact is, I had never planned to write his biography. It was the story of my mother which I thought was far more fascinating that I would turn into a book one day. However in November 2018, Lindsey Davis, director of development at Bradford Grammar School emailed me to say that some of the old boys had reached out to the school suggesting celebrations for his hundredth birthday. Lindsey asked me to send her a timeline of my father's life. When I started writing it in January 2019 it got bigger and bigger and then it got so big, I just couldn't stop and I had to tell the story, the whole story; the good and the bad, and turn it into the book you have in your hands.

My mother always overshadowed my father and even in this book it is difficult to tell his story without frequently mentioning her as their lives were inextricably entwined. It is also difficult to tell his story without telling mine as the words on these pages are often about my memories of him. I hope to have done him justice by finally revealing the man behind the charismatic woman, the man who also had charisma, it was just that I didn't know it.

It is his old boys from Bradford Grammar School who revealed that side of him to me with their stories of his passionate teaching in the classroom where one of them even described him as being a 'showman'. My father a showman? How could that be possible? You only have to read the old boys' messages and quotes to find out why.

I have enjoyed writing his biography. It has been an emotional trip down memory lane and many times I shed a tear or two but I also laughed. I hope you enjoy discovering my father too and his fascinating life. His life was quite extraordinary for such a seemingly ordinary man. But you will soon find out that he wasn't exactly ordinary by any means.

ACKNOWLEDGEMENTS

I have a lot of people to thank who have helped to make the writing and publishing of this biography possible. In the first place I want to thank Lindsey Davis, the development director of Bradford Grammar School. She was the person to inspire me to write this book although neither she nor I knew it at the time.

The biggest thanks go to my dearest and oldest friend, Amanda Leonard-Myers, for the initial proofreading. She and I went to school together, to St. Joseph's College, the then direct-grant Catholic Grammar school adjacent to Bradford Grammar School. The years have passed but our friendship remains the same. At a distance, she lives in Devon and I live in Madrid, Amanda has encouraged me from the start and has been there on every step of the journey. In a way we have done this project together and it would not be the biography you have in your hands today if it hadn't been for her help and moral support. She was part of my childhood, knew my parents and family so well that they were like second parents to her. So who better could I have had to help me on this remarkable journey?

Since I started the biography it has been a fascinating journey into my father's and my own past. I have been in touch with the institutions my father was most linked to in his life, from his school to retirement. Each one of them, Clifton College, Selwyn College Cambridge and Bradford Grammar School have not only responded enthusiastically from the very beginning but have bent over backwards to help me. They provided me with a lot of the photos illustrating this biography, photos we had never seen before. They have been a mine of information too about dates, names and places. I am eternally grateful to them. In particular I must thank Tim Greene, headmaster of Clifton College for his enthusiasm from the beginning. His colleague, Jeremy Pickles, the director of development for the school, unearthed all sorts of photos which have hugely enhanced this biography, particularly my father's school report from 1935. Their offer to fly the flag from the Wilson Tower on 1 May 2019 the day he turned a hundred is the biggest homage they could pay him. Roger Mosey, Master of Selwyn College, Cambridge and also an ex-pupil of Bradford Grammar School, jumped on board as soon as I wrote to him. He put me in the hands of the college archivist, Elizabeth Stratton and she provided me with exact dates as well as the lovely photo of my father on Matriculation Day in 1938. They even sent out their development manager to visit him, their oldest living pupil. My father was thrilled with Erin Bond's visit in April 2019. I also want to thank the Royal Navy Association for responding so kindly and sending my father a card from his beloved navy. Thank you Nigel Huxtable for your positive response. Ana Nowak from the Royal Navy Disclosure Team very kindly sent me perhaps the most valuable material for this biography, my father's personal war records. Jennifer Thorpe, the archivist of New College Oxford, very kindly provided me with information on my grandfather's time as a chorister in Oxford for which I am very grateful. Thanks go too to the Norwegian Ambassador in Madrid, the Honorable Helge Skaara for his role in making sure King Harold V sent a card, via direct contact with the King's private secretary, Anja Torvund who in turn got the King to sign it.

I also have to acknowledge the role his 'old boys' from Bradford Grammar School have played in helping to write their former teacher's story. Many of them have reached out to him, through me, over the years and I am in touch with quite a few of them. They always tell me what an amazing teacher he was and how much he influenced their lives. Through them I have seen another side of my father, a side I never saw at home. In many ways they too have inspired me to write this biography and some of their comments have helped to make it much more entertaining. So thanks David Whitlam, Jon Starkey, Michael Forte, James Crookes, Andy Myers and especially Simon Hewitt who really opened my eyes about my father, the teacher in class, a very important part of the man I wouldn't have known otherwise. And thanks to all of you who reached out.

Simon Hewitt provided the invaluable Clarence Quotes he compiled at school during classes with my father. They are hilarious and show exactly the sort of teacher he was - quite remarkable really. Simon also helped by revising the initial manuscript. His advice and help are much appreciated.

People encouraged me on the way. I have to thank our lodger, Andrew Prior who is from Scotland. Andrew, being interested in my father's experience in the war, sat down with him one day when we were away in Montrondo and started getting the initial information I needed to continue. He got out of my father the names of some of his ships and much more. Thanks to Andy I persevered, badgering my father with questions slowly over lunch for weeks on end and in the afternoons until the picture was complete. I am also indebted to him for one of the juiciest quotes in the biography about the best way to learn Russian.

Barry Hillier, a trustee of the Holyhead Maritime Museum would become important in the making of this book. He had written a story on my father's great grandfather, John Collins which we found on the web. I immediately wrote to him and he provided me with some very valuable documents for the project. All the information about my ancestors linked to Anglesey come from him. Above all, it is thanks to him that we found my father's youngest uncle, Owen Noel Lloyd. Barry has proved to be a mine of information and such a willing helper that I don't have the words to express what his help has meant to me. After all he didn't even know me. Thank you Barry, for your invaluable help and for your time.

When I thought I had finished the biography there were a few question marks about long lost ancestors of my father's. It was then that our family friend, and my father and mother's past pupil, Andrew Dale, from the Norwich Russian courses, stepped in and lent a hand. He searched the web exhaustively and filled in nearly all the blanks I had. Not only did he fill in the blanks, he took on the work of creating a whole family tree of the Lloyd family for my father's hundredth birthday and making a beautiful book out of it too. Andy searched high and low for my father's long-lost cousins in Scotland, the descendants of my grandfather, and found them. I cannot thank him enough. I have to add that it was great fun working with him. Together with Barry he was my most important genealogist.

I must not forget either to thank the girls from my events agency QuintaEsencia for the wonderful work they did to produce the poster of the family tree. Thank you Bea, Gloria, Cristina and Angela, especially, for doing the creative work. I am also sorry for the many times I kept having to change it as new ancestors were found. It looks beautiful in the frame in our home now.

Thanks should also be given to the Spanish company Habemus Estudio who designed the cover and helped me self publish the book so there would be copies on time for my father's birthday and in particular to Mikel Escalara. It wasn't easy for his company to work with a manuscript in English but they did a great job.

And a special mention goes to Joanne Wilcock who ended up being part of the whole project. Joanne is a teacher of French and Spanish from Lancashire who was my Airbnb guest in January 2019. She was fascinated by my father's story. So when I sent her the very first manuscript it was her feedback that encouraged me to include more about my father's involvement in the war and more facts about his life. I took her advice and am very grateful. Joanne was so interested in the story she set about researching Courtenay's father's past, even visiting his old house, lodgings and churches where he was a curate in Anglesey. She even searched for long-lost cousins who are still alive but we had lost contact with. Thanks to her the two final pieces of the puzzle that would complete the family tree were found. With determination and perseverance she singlehandedly found my father's first cousin, Angela Benson and his cousin Mona's daughter, Jennifer. I would never have found either of them without her. Above all I appreciate her interest and her enthusiasm.

I also have to thank my husband Eladio who has borne with me while writing and working on the story of my father's life and my memories of him. He was not part of our past but he has encouraged me all the way. I also want to thank my daughters, Suzy and Oli who dote on their grandfather for their interest in his story.

I should not forget either the role L.R, Price Publications have played in publishing this book. They believed in me from the beginning for which I am eternally grateful. Thank you Russell Spencer for your part in making a dream come true; the publication of this book in my home country.

And finally I want to thank my own father for his help. He is one hundred years old and has a remarkable memory but I pestered him with questions for a long time and it was difficult for him because he is very hard of hearing. I told him I was sorry for badgering him so much and the dear man replied, 'Oh but I like being badgered'. He was very eager to help always. However, at one point, when I asked him about a certain Uncle David or David Collins Esquire who in 1889 got a medal from the then King of Siam, he replied, 'It's a bit difficult to remember things from a hundred years ago'. Indeed it is but he has done a splendid job. Again, I only wish I had listened to him when he spoke about his life and the war when I was younger. But I'm so glad I have listened now when it is still not too late and I hope I've got it right. This is not a history book. Not everything I record is completely accurate as memories fade. It is a book about the life of my father, so if there are any mistakes, historians and sticklers, please forgive me. Daddy, thank you for your patience and I hope you like the biography and all the surprises you had for your hundredth birthday. As I said to you recently, they are all gone; your parents, Raymond, Gloria, her children, Mummy, George, Aunty Masha. Only you and I are left now so it gives me enormous satisfaction to bring them back to life if only on these pages.

INTRODUCTION

Charles Courtenay Lloyd, unusually, uses his middle name, Courtenay, as his first name. His maternal grandfather's name was Charles so maybe the family used Courtenay so as to distinguish the two. In any case it was always quite confusing for everyone, as Courtenay is more often a surname. Also, his name is often misspelled and written as 'Courtney' rather than 'Courtenay'. His immediate family called him 'Court', it being his maternal grandmother who first called him that. So I will refer to him in this biography as 'Courtenay Lloyd', 'my father' or just 'Courtenay' as he was always known.

He is described in his school report as 'dreamy' and someone who found it 'difficult to express his feelings', but overall 'a perfectly reliable boy'. This is indeed true of him. The teacher who wrote that 84 years ago could probably never have envisaged the man he would become and the life he would lead; or maybe he guessed it as he also wrote at the end, 'He left too young for one to be able to judge whether he would develop any leadership but were signs that he might do'. What the teacher failed to notice is that he is above all a positive person who looks on the bright side of life.

Primarily, my father is an intellectual and an academic; the quintessential English gentleman. However, as those who know him would agree, beyond his modest exterior lies a formidable intellect. He may be given to the occasional outburst of anger but only when the occasion merits it.

He is a polyglot who, in addition to his native tongue, still speaks and reads in Russian, Norwegian, German, French and Spanish. His great loves in life, apart from travelling and languages, are nature (he was an enthusiastic walker and, except during the war, never drove a car),

COURTENAY LLOYD IN HIS STUDY BY HIS MAPS -
HEATON GROVE, BRADFORD 1973.

geography, modern history, especially the Second World War, and the life and times of the world's late dictators. Posters of them decorated the walls of his study at his home of 40 years at 6 Heaton Grove, Bradford. Also decorating these walls was a huge Russian-made map of Europe, as well as maps of Finland, Iceland and Spain.

He is a great lover of the Nordic countries and is quite fluent in Danish and Swedish. He also has a smattering of Dutch and even Finnish and Icelandic. These are the languages of the countries he loves nearly as much as Norway, his favourite nation. He had a collection of shortwave radios and loved to listen to classical music and programmes from all over Europe. He hated so-called 'pop music' which he said was for the musically illiterate. He told his pupils, 'When I am free, I don't spend the evening watching tripe. My God no! I twiddle the knobs on my short wave Hungarian radio. It's music, you know, not like Radio Luxembourg!' For this biography I quizzed him on his favourite music and he enthusiastically said, 'Oh, Johann Strauss, not very classical though'. I asked him what he meant and he said well he liked classical music but was not very musically erudite so Strauss and his waltzes suited him beautifully.

Usually the first pages he turns to, still today, when reading a newspaper, are those that feature the weather forecast, another of his great passions. He told his pupils at Bradford Grammar School that it was 'a scandal that we don't have our radio weather forecasts read with poetry. They're so deadpan… it's an absolute disgrace!' But there's poetry about the shipping forecast. I enjoy that. I'd love to receive world temperatures from the Met Office through the post'.

I've never known him to have many friends. He may sometimes seem a bit like a hermit and often travelled abroad alone. But he has a very rich inner life and above all is a family man. He was always there for all of us. I particularly remember our correspondence when I was at university and in my year abroad in Madrid. He would write to me unfailingly once a week and I would write back to him immediately. I think I mostly asked him for money. My mother hardly ever wrote; it was always him. I still have all our letters and I treasure them.

He may sound boring but he isn't. It's just that his mind races all over the place while he is dreaming, maybe thinking about his beloved Norway or some pretty wild flowers he has found on his walk or the book he is reading about a Scottish island. He does not have a sense of humour as such but rather a sense of fun. I think it was the fun side of my mother which attracted him to her, and her ability to show her feelings. With him she could get away with murder. In the early 1960s when dishwashers first came out, my mother, ever the more progressive one in their marriage, wanted to buy one. Never liking change, he threatened her with divorce if she bought one. Needless to say, she bought one and their marriage continued semi peacefully. Like most men he always put the heating down. My mother would then surreptitiously turn it up. Thus our house went from cold to hot and from hot to cold continuously.

The image of Courtenay as a goody-goody when he was young is slightly tarnished by him once having tied together the shoelaces of the lady who was in a queue in front of him and his mother at a post office.

He still possesses a keen memory and entered his hundredth year, although living a quieter life, still reading books in different languages, mostly historical as well as the English and Spanish newspapers, The *Daily Telegraph* and *El País*, every day. He never reads 'bestsellers', his interest in books being far more high-brow. The bookcases in his room and study in Madrid today are full of the whole works of Russian literature in Russian, a myriad of tourist guides to various Scandinavian countries published in the 1930s and 1940s, history books, and books of military events. His favourite Russian author is Anton Chekhov and his favourite British author is Charlotte Brontë. He also has countless dictionaries and atlases. One of them is so big it's impossible to hold in one hand. He got it from a German prisoner of war who was in Oslo and about to return to his home country. Apparently he had too much luggage to carry it and my father snapped it out of his hands very gratefully! It has got the German names for towns in former Czechoslovakia. He told his pupils, 'I spend hours pleasantly thumbing through it'.

The pictures of the late dictators of Europe have all gone. Instead there hangs a big portrait of Tsar Nicholas II which used to grace our dining room in prime position in Bradford. He told me recently it was given to my mother by her uncle Sasha Stachovich, her mother's brother, who brought it out of Russia when the family fled the Revolution and went to live in Paris. For him the dictators of today are the likes of Nicolas Maduro, Vladimir Putin and Kim Jong-un. The only novels on these shelves are from classical literature. I'm not sure if he still has it but one of his most prized books was a Russo-Sanskrit etymological dictionary which he often referred to when teaching. He loves etymology, the origin of words, as well as names and locations of towns. As children we learned nearly all the capital cities, at least in Europe. He used to make George and I compete and, aged about 5, I had to learn to spell Reykjavik and I always got it wrong. I still do.

Afternoons are spent watching the news on the BBC every day and he remains keenly interested in all that is going on around him and in the wider world. He has a hearty appetite and enjoys home-cooked healthy meals with the family which always include a small glass of Rioja daily and often a piece of chocolate - he always had a sweet tooth. For a man of his age he is in very good health and state of mind.

I told him I thought he had had a fascinating life. He replied, 'A very enjoyable life, I think'. In short my father is a person who enjoys the small pleasures of life and is a very positive person.

My father taught me to look on the bright side and to enjoy the small pleasures in life. I remember as a child going with him to Manchester on the train from Bradford to that even darker industrial town in the north of England, to see the dentist, Mr. Car, a friend of my parents. I pointed out how ugly a street was and my father said that he always looked for the beautiful things and that very often there was something beautiful to be found in or around ugly things. I have practised his philosophy nearly always and it has held me in good stead.

Courtenay Lloyd is also someone who has lost nearly everyone dear to him in his life including his two siblings Raymond and Gloria, his wife and latterly his son George. Yet he has always suffered in silence, stoically soldiering on, reading *The Times* and *The Telegraph and Argus* when he lived in Bradford, reading books, going to the library, taking his walks, enjoying his food and all the good things in life.

As a child there was a picture above his bed of a fawn and the words: 'Be a good beast, suffer in silence'. Not being a very demonstrative person, he always quietly followed these words, although beneath his innate shyness and modesty lie a heart of gold and a very good and gentle man.

I

YOUTH

1919 - 1939

COURTENAY ABOUT TO TURN 14, RAYMOND AGED 10, AND GLORIA AGED 6. BRISTOL MAY 1933. BOTH BOYS ARE WEARING THEIR CLIFTON COLLEGE SCHOOL UNIFORM

HIS PARENTS ON THEIR WEDDING DAY 15 JANUARY 1918. NOTICE THE WWI CHAPLAIN UNIFORM OF HIS FATHER. THEY WERE MARRIED AT THE OLD CHURCH ST. NICHOLAS, UPHILL (NEAR WESTON-SUPER-MARE) AND WENT ON HONEYMOON TO CLEVEDON.

YOUTH
1919 - 1939

Charles Courtenay Lloyd was born on 1 May 1919, in Amington near Tamworth (Staffordshire today but formerly County Warwick). He was the first son of the Reverend Canon John Collins Lloyd, born in Holyhead Anglesey, Wales; and Dorothy Gertrude Scull, an accomplished pianist, born in Attingham (Atcham). (See APPENDIX II for information about his immediate family and ancestors).

I asked my father to describe his father for this biography and he answered that he was a man of many talents. When pressed, he added he was a popular vicar as he was very sympathetic to his parishioners. I then asked him if he thought his father had been a good father to him. His answer: 'I never thought differently'. I asked the same question about his mother. He said she was talented too as she was a piano player and was a Licentiate of the Royal Academy of Music, something he much admired as he never learned to play the piano. He also said that his mother was not a 'disciplinarian' which I was happy to hear.

Courtenay's siblings were younger brother Raymond Lloyd (born in Edstaston, Shrewsbury) who sadly died of 'infantile paralysis' (polio) aged 16 on 15 October in 1938, and his younger sister Gloria Lloyd (born Sledmere, East Yorkshire) who died in 1971 in an air crash in Rijeka (in former Yugoslavia) with all her family.

The family lived at the rectories in Amington (near Tamworth in Staffordshire) and later in Edstaston (Shrewsbury), Sledmere (the former East Riding of Yorkshire), and in Henbury (five miles from Bristol) where Courtenay Lloyd's father was a Church of England vicar, later made a canon at St. Mary's Church.

As children they would holiday at the seaside in Weston-super-Mare where Courtenay's maternal grandmother lived. The house where she went to live after her husband, Charles Edward Scull, died was called 'Sundorne' and is on 22 Charlton Road. While writing this book it was on sale for more than £400,000.

The boys loved playing cricket and there are photos of them playing together on the beach and at home. My father well remembers family summer holidays in his father's native Anglesey with his cousins, Mona, William, Blodwen and Gwen. He told me the beach they most went to was at Trearddur Bay.

For this biography, thankfully, I have had a great resource in the family photos my father has kept over the years. Quite a few were taken in the gardens at the vicarage in Henbury where the family lived for the longest period of time. Here is one of the whole family together; from left to right: his father, mother, Aunty Gwen (his mother's only sister), his sister Gloria, his brother Raymond and himself aged about 12. They look a happy bunch.

MY FATHER WITH HIS FAMILY AND AUNT GWEN. HENBURY c.1931. MY FATHER IS THE LITTLE BOY SITTING ON A CHAIR.

COURTENAY'S FATHER, REVD. JOHN
COLLINS LLOYD STANDING BY THE
SOUTH PORCH AT ST. MARY'S CHURCH IN
HENBURY. THIS ENTRANCE IS ONLY USED
THESE DAYS FOR WEDDINGS.

COURTENAY'S MATERNAL
GRANDMOTHER'S HOUSE IN
WESTON-SUPER-MARE.

My grandparents must have invested in a modern camera of the era as there are many photos taken in the gardens at the vicarage in Henbury. When Courtenay's father was appointed to St. Mary's Church, Henbury in 1928, the old vicarage was in no state to live in so a new one was built on Station Road especially for them. The family moved into this brand new vicarage and they all loved it. I asked my father why he loved the vicarage and he answered because it was so modern. He also told me he shared a bedroom with his brother Raymond. I was very disturbed to read that in the summer of 2018 the house was burned down by vandals. It felt like the final blow of a curse on the family after all they had endured.

St. Mary's Church at Henbury was where Courtenay's father spent the most part of his career and from where he retired in 1957. Upon retirement, his parents went to live in Ickenham (on the outskirts of London and in Middlesex) to live near their daughter Gloria.

Talking about his early life, my father recently told me he remembered Bristol well before the German bombardments called the Bristol Blitz. He particularly remembers walking along Wine Street towards the High

Street where there was a 'picturesque house called The Dutch House'. I looked it up on the internet and indeed there was. It was a timber-framed building and a well-known landmark of the city until it was destroyed in 1940. Bristol was a target for the German Luftwaffe because of its port and the Bristol Aeroplane Company. It was the fifth most heavily bombed city in WWII.

HENBURY VICARAGE ON STATION ROAD.

RAYMOND, GLORIA AND COURTENAY WITH THEIR FATHER c. 1930.

SCHOOL. CLIFTON COLLEGE BRISTOL
1928 - 1935

He and his brother Raymond attended Clifton College in Bristol where they received a solid early education. The day houses are all called towns, North Town, East Town, West Town and South Town. Courtenay and Raymond were in North Town which my father remembers very well. Founded in 1862, Clifton College is one of the original 26 public schools as defined by the Public Schools Yearbook in 1889.

It has an illustrious history and is one of England's most prestigious schools. The school has some very famous alumni which include Field Marshall Douglas Haig.

A contemporary of my father was Trevor Howard, the British actor. Other famous Old Cliftonians are Michael Redgrave and John Cleese. I think my father has always been shyly and secretly proud of having attended such a prestigious English public school. It also has strong links with WWII, becoming at one point the US First Army HQ. After WWII, General Eisenhower donated a US flag to the school for its efforts in the war.

Ever since, Clifton College has flown that flag once

CLIFTON COLLEGE BRISTOL WHERE MY FATHER
AND HIS BROTHER WENT TO SCHOOL.

a year on 4 July, Independence Day. On 1 May 2019, on the occasion of my father's one-hundredth birthday the OC (Old Cliftonian) flag was flown for him which is a very rare occurrence and a great honour. The school also sang happy birthday to him from the chapel.

Latin was one of my father's favourite subjects which would help him later when he became a linguist. He got a thorough grounding in the dead language as did his future wife, my mother, and often both of them uttered quotes in Latin at home and made my brother and I feel quite ignorant.

While interviewing him for this biography, he recalled the inscription in Latin on the tower of his father's church, St. Mary's in Henbury. He spelled it out to his far less cultured daughter: *Pulvis et umbra sumus*. I checked whether this was right with my husband Eladio who, having learned Latin while studying to be a priest is an expert. While studying, all Eladio's subjects were taught in Latin. Indeed, this phrase or saying meaning 'we are dust and shadow' is correct and apparently comes from Horace. That was pretty amazing for someone aged ninety-nine, about to become a hundred. His knowledge of Latin is still intact, clever man.

PHOTO FROM HIS CLIFTON COLLEGE RECORD 1933. SOURCE CLIFTON COLLEGE ARCHIVES

Courtenay told me the headmaster at the time was a man called Mr. Whatley. He was good at languages from the very beginning and at the school he was awarded the Hilman Modern Languages prize for French. I asked him about the prize and he modestly said it was an award given every year and that he was given a book but had no idea who Mr. Hilman was. However, because of the Great Depression after the Wall Street Crash, when Courtenay Lloyd was 16, his father, very wrongly, thought it better to take him out of school and find him a job. Through an influential parishioner, he entered the Imperial Tobacco Company. The influential parishioner was no less

AT CLIFTON COLLEGE BRISTOL 1933 WITH HIS NORTH TOWN FELLOW PUPILS AND TEACHERS. FRONT ROW THIRD FROM THE LEFT SITTING CROSS-LEGGED.

than the general manager of the company. I suspect it was quite prestigious to work at Wills and his father thought he might have a life career there. But he didn't and went on to do greater things.

Clifton College also unearthed his overall school report from 1928, covering the time that he entered until April 1935 when he left, one month before his sixteenth birthday. The first entry says 'dreamy' which he was and always has been. Then appears several times the fact that he found it 'difficult to express his feelings' which is certainly true. Overall he was quite good at school except for maths and science which figures. For Latin he gets good marks. In the final summary the teacher who wrote the report is spot on. He wrote: 'Left young to go into a post in "Wills". He was quite good at most of his subjects with one or two marked weaknesses. He was not athletic, but could be a quite reasonable performer when he put himself to it. He left too young for one to be able to judge whether he would develop any leadership but were signs that he might do'. It ends: 'A perfectly reliable boy'. I think the teacher was spot on in his description. You can read the full report in Appendix III. I showed my father the report as soon as I got it. He chuckled when I told him it said he was 'dreamy'.

COURTENAY LLOYD AGED 15 AT CLIFTON COLLEGE BRISTOL IN 1934, HIS LAST SCHOOL PHOTO.

When he was taken out of school in the middle of term in April 1935, he told me he felt a little bewildered. I insisted on knowing why he was taken out and his answer was the economic situation. He still has the Clifton College cricket jumper he wore at school. Now rather tattered, he has kept it always, perhaps out of nostalgia, and wears it still today if he is cold.

WILLS – IMPERIAL TOBACCO COMPANY
1935 – 1938

Courtenay Lloyd joined the Imperial Tobacco Company in 1935. Founded by Wills, Watkins & Co in 1786, it was commonly known as Wills. When my father joined it had already been taken over and become part of the Imperial Tobacco Company with seven other British tobacco companies but, in Bristol, at least it was still called 'Wills'. My father remembers that two of the other brands were *Players* and *Ogdens*. He told me he felt very junior when he began but that his bosses were quite kind to him.

He loved his time there where his main task was to collect the news of the company from different newspapers from around the world. Thus his interest in languages and geography was forged. He also received a free carton of cigarettes once a week but was never a real smoker although smoking in those days was very common and the dangers of nicotine would only be discovered decades later.

With his earnings he travelled extensively abroad before WWII to places like Geneva, Belgium, Germany and Scandinavia and still today talks about these trips remembering the exact dates he travelled. His first trip abroad was to Belgium with his mother in 1935 and his second trip to Germany and former Czechoslovakia with her again the following year. He visited the Black Forest, Cologne, and Berlin. I asked him if he could notice how Germany was becoming Nazified from his trips there and he said very much so and that there was Nazi propaganda everywhere. But ever the optimist, he added that at the time he thought it would all blow over as, indeed, many people thought but of course it didn't.

On most of his trips he went with his mother and he said families didn't go abroad on holiday together in those days and that his father had his duties as a vicar to attend to. I asked him whether his mother liked travelling. He said he wasn't sure but that she went with him because she thought travelling abroad would be good for his studies. I also asked him what sparked his interest in languages and he says he thinks it was by chance and from reading newspapers.

He still has a book by the famous German author Theodor Storm that he bought in Berlin in 1938 when he was aged just nineteen. The novella, *Immensee* was the book that brought fame to the nineteenth-century German author. About a year ago I discovered him rereading it and was astonished to see it was written in German gothic script. Undoubtedly, Theodor Storm would think Courtenay Lloyd was immense too.

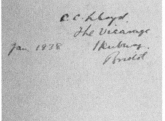

IMMENSEE BY THEODOR STORM, A BOOK COURTENAY LLOYD
BOUGHT IN BERLIN IN 1938, PRINTED IN GOTHIC SCRIPT
WHICH HE STILL READS TODAY.

DEATH OF RAYMOND
October 15 1938 Weston-Super-Mare

Tragedy struck the family when Courtenay's younger brother Raymond fell ill, aged 16. He had all the symptoms of a bad bout of flu and was taken to stay by the sea with his grandmother in Weston-super- Mare, and kept in isolation in case anyone caught the infection. It turned out to be the dreaded disease polio, commonly known then as 'infantile paralysis' for which there was no vaccine in the 1930s.

Raymond was a sunny boy, different in character to 'Court' and far more practically minded than his older brother who preferred his books. Raymond relished all things mechanical and once even took his father's car apart and then put it all back together again.

Raymond was very good with his hands unlike my father. The most Courtenay could manage when we lived in Bradford, that I remember, was how to change a plug or a bulb but not much else I'm afraid.

Raymond was always referred to as 'Ray' or 'Uncle Raymond', and Courtenay, to this day, has

EDSTASTON

THE DEATH occurred last week, after an acute attack of infantile paralysis, of Raymond Lloyd, aged 16, younger son of the Rev. and Mrs. J. C. Lloyd, Henbury Vicarage, Bristol. Educated at Clifton College, Raymond Lloyd was born at Edstaston Vicarage, where his father (a former curate of St. Mary's, Shrewsbury) was vicar from 1920 to 1924. Mrs. Lloyd is a daughter of the late Mr. C. E. Scull, Abbey Foregate, Shrewsbury, and Mrs. Scull, Weston-super-Mare.

PRESS CLIPPING ANNOUNCING RAYMOND'S DEATH.

RAYMOND LLOYD,
COURTENAY'S BROTHER, AGED
16, THE YEAR HE DIED OF POLIO
(1938). THIS IS THE PICTURE
COURTENAY HAS ALWAYS HAD
ON HIS DESK.

a photo of him on his desk. My mother told me the only time he ever cried was when his brother died but I'm not sure that is true.

When I asked my father to describe his brother for this book, he told me Ray was very different to him and that he was quite independent.

When I got in touch with Clifton College Bristol for this biography, the very kind Director of Development, Jeremy Pickles, found his school registry number (10545) and told me his entry is very short. 'Born 5/8/22 brother, North Town. Left in the third term of 1937. Died 1938'.

He cheered me up enormously when he sent a photo of Raymond with his fellow 'chums' of North Town taken in 1932 when he would have been ten years old. It is lovely to be able to include the photo in my father's biography. It makes it more complete. My father was astounded when he saw the photo and immediately recognized his brother. He said: 'Oh, good Lord, there is Raymond.'

RAYMOND AGED 10 AT CLIFTON COLLEGE NT 1932(circled in red).

SELWYN COLLEGE CAMBRIDGE
1938 - 1939

Courtenay Lloyd forewent his formal education far too early in life for someone who would turn out to be such an intellectual and distinguished linguist. Being a keen student, he kept up his studies by attending night classes and just before World War II broke out earned a place at Selwyn College, Cambridge to read Modern Languages. Selwyn College had a strong relationship with the Church of England and was the obvious choice for the son of a vicar. He also told me Selwyn College was the

SELWYN COLLEGE CAMBRIDGE (PHOTO BY DAVID ILIFF).

choice too because it was a religious college. I asked him if he was religious at the time. He hesitated in answering me. First he said that because of his upbringing he was expected to be so. When I insisted, he said, 'Yes, I suppose I was religious'. I think he still is as every time one of us undergoes an operation, however minor, he always tells me, 'I prayed for you', bless him.

Funnily enough it was his father who suggested he went to study at Cambridge. I asked why again, if it had been his father who had taken him out of school. His answer was because he was showing a great interest in languages. I also asked him how he got in and he replied quite unabashedly: 'Oh through the old boys' system I suppose!' It must have been through his father's relationship with the church. Courtenay chose to read French and German until the war interrupted his studies. When he returned after the war he transferred to German and Scandinavian languages, majoring in Norwegian. When Erin Bond, the college Alumni relations manager, visited my father in Madrid in April 2019 she brought with her the original photo of his matriculation in 1938 as well as two prints of the college. He looked at them all with great interest. After finding himself in the photo, he also found two fellow students. One was a friend called Hollwey with whom he told us he once cycled all the way from Cambridge to Bristol. He also recognized another student, Claus H.E. Brauer who he told us was German. That of course interested him as he was a studying German. He remembered all the buildings of the college, pointing out the chapel and telling us that when attending service they had to wear a white surplice. No doubt attending service at Selwyn was obligatory at the time because of its connection with the Church of England. He told us that the Chaplain was called Revd. A.C. Blythe, that the administrator was someone called J.P. Durrant and that the Master of the College was George Armitage Chase, who was also a bishop. My father also remembered that his room was on staircase F7 which Erin told me is in the main courtyard and that his 'bedder' or 'gyp' (college servant) was called Freddy Fromint. Considering he was talking about events that happened over 80 years ago, that is an awful lot of information to remember. His memory is quite remarkable. At Cambridge, as at school, he was the perfect undergraduate taking his studies seriously. He never considered it anything special to have studied at Cambridge University and I suspect he found his years as a student there quite normal too. He was no party animal and was ever the conscientious gentleman. My mother only ever saw him drunk once in his life and I never did, although there was nothing like a glass of vodka in the company of extrovert Russians to bring a sparkle to his shy blue eyes.

COURTENAY LLOYD AT CAMBRIDGE UNIVERSITY. MATRICULATION 1938. MY FATHER IS IN THE SECOND ROW AND THE SECOND PERSON FROM THE LEFT.

II

WAR AND POST-WAR
1940 - 1948

WWII CONSCRIPTION. JOINING THE NAVY
1940

When WW2 broke out on 1st September 1939, my father who was just 20 at the time, found himself in Sweden on holiday. He had just finished his first year at Cambridge and went hitchhiking in Scandinavia. Hitchhiking was very customary in those days he told me.

He had returned to the youth hostel in the small town of Åre in Sweden where he was staying and that was when he heard the news. I asked him what his reaction was.

He told me gravely that he had alarming memories of his father's descriptions of the horrors of WW1 and his hope then was that they would not be transferred to this new war. He had no idea then that he would be witness to what would become the deadliest military conflict in history. His immediate thoughts were that he must return home but it wasn't easy.

He hitchhiked to Bergen in Norway and there were lots of passing cars but they were nearly all full. He told me he cried out to them in Swedish "Har du plats I bilen?" (Do you have room in your car?) and that the answer was nearly always "Nej".

In the end, three different cars picked him up and he finally made it to Bergen where he went straight to see the British Consul. There were quite a few stranded British citizens like him that the Consul repatriated to England by boat cost free he told me.

Once back in Bristol and because of the war, there was no question of returning to Cambridge. He had to sign up as did most young men of his age.

His father suggested he join the Royal Navy, the RNVR at the time, thinking it would be safer than the other forces.

I wondered why if the war broke out in September 1939 he didn't sign up until January 1940. He explained that it was because of the "inevitable delays in signing up". In any case on 8 January 1940 he joined as an ordinary seaman.

On 8 January 1940 he joined as an ordinary seaman. After three months training at the R.N. Barracks, Devonport, he was drafted to his first ship, the HMS *Norfolk*. He could never have known at the time how important Norway would become to him and that it would be his first ship, the HMS Norfolk, that would carry the King of Norway, Haakon VII, and his family from exile in England, back to Oslo in June 1945. Nor would he have believed that he would be given a medal from the Norwegian King for his contribution to the liberation of that country from the Nazi invasion or that he would be instrumental in helping the country back on its feet.

I asked him what his role was on the ship and he said, 'Oh you know, obeying orders'. He told me he remembered that the commander was Captain Philipps. He must have done quite a good job though as he was soon promoted to able seaman.

After doing an officers' course on HMS *King Alfred* at Hove, near Brighton, he became a sub lieutenant in November 1940. In May 1943 he was promoted to lieutenant. In letters to his sister Gloria it is obvious he didn't think much of Brighton at all.

He was stationed for most of the war in Scotland. Orkney was the main royal naval base for the Atlantic. Scotland and the Scottish Islands are another of his great loves and he has always spoken fondly of the Hebrides, the Outer Hebrides, the Orkneys and the Shetlands. The story goes that when he went aboard his first ship, he greeted an older seaman who was cleaning the decks and said, 'The navy makes a man of you', to which the seaman replied in a broad cockney accent:

LT. COURTENAY LLOYD, SCOTLAND 1942
ABOUT TO BOARD HMS *WELLS*

'It makes a f****** monkey of you!' But the seaman was wrong, the navy made a man of my father. My mother gleefully used to tell everyone that her husband, a clergyman's son of genteel extraction, took his pyjamas on board with him to the great amusement of his fellow shipmates. She even told us he got down on his knees to pray on the first night to more amusement which was something he never did again. Another story she liked to tell was that it was his job to give out the 'French letters' to the seamen when they arrived at a port but didn't know what he was giving out! He soon learned the game though and began to love the sea and the navy, a love which would last a lifetime.

COURTENAY LLOYD ON BOARD HMS *WELLS* IN WWII 1940.

'I had a lucky war,' he says, referring to the fact that neither of the two ships he most remembers, the HMS *Wells* nor the HMS *Mansfield*, both destroyers and originally belonging to the US Navy, were ever attacked. The mission of both ships was to chase and destroy German U-boats.

His first ship after becoming an officer was the HMS *Mansfield*. On HMS *Mansfield* which was loaned to the exiled Norwegian Navy he was a liaison officer. As the only British officer on board he began to learn Norwegian. He was now passing messages and instructions from the British Admiralty to the Norwegian Navy and back, coding and decoding them as necessary. The commander of HMS *Mansfield* was Captain Ulstrup. Courtenay remembers other Norwegian officers on board too: Holst,

Haug and Fjellheim. He remembers their ship's greatest achievement, the raiding of a fish-oil factory in German hands at Øksfjord near Hammerfest.

Fish oil was apparently used by the Germans for the manufacture of explosives so this was an important mission. The raid was successful but unfortunately the owner, a Norwegian quisling (traitor), got away. Later the locals gave out postcards to the officers of the ship saying 'takk for besøket' meaning 'Thank you for the visit'. As he spells that out for me, he tells me to put the forward stroke across the 'o' and says the 'ø' in Norwegian sounds like 'eu' (as in the French word 'fleur') He remembers the snow-covered mountains when they landed at Øksfjord. Again he tells me the 'o' has a stroke across it as he spells out the name of the fjord. His descriptions of the beauty of this area later inspired his own father to take a trip to Norway to visit it sometime later.

From HMS *Mansfield*, Courtenay was drafted to HMS *Wells* as the signals and C.B. officer. He remembers that the commander was Captain Lee. No doubt Captain Lee would remember him too as he wrote in one of his reports about my father: 'He is somewhat solitary by nature and though popular with his messmates, prefers to go ashore by himself'. I laughed when I read that as it is just like him. Captain Lee has some good things to say about him but writes, 'He has taken a great deal of interest in signal duties, but suffers from a lack of ability to concentrate and organize. He is a pleasant character, full of good humour under normal circumstance but has fits of intense depression whenever he feels that he has failed in any respect. He is naturally slow thinking, but once an idea is fixed in his head he holds on to it'. It wasn't exactly a glowing report. However, if I think about it, my father was only 21 at the time and hadn't been an officer for long. Who would be good at concentrating and organization at that age? As to getting upset about failing in something, that is just my father who only ever wants to please. The slow thinking is a trait of his but that's because he thinks a lot before he speaks and always has. As to the idea fixed in his head, well my father always was a little bit stubborn although he has mellowed a lot in his old age. In a later report Captain Lee writes: 'It is thought that with experience he may gain self-confidence and become more methodical'. I was relieved to see that in his future reports he improved by leaps and bounds.

The captain on HMS Lancaster in his final report writes: 'Has considerable personal charm. Is well educated and intelligent. A good messmate. Has a good power of command, is a smart spoken Divisional Officer'.

No doubt he worked as hard as possible to be rewarded with this praise. Vice Admiral Harwood writes of his time with HMS *Proserpine*: 'An executive officer who has been working for some months in the familiar realm of intelligence. He has quickly made himself at home and mastered the essentials. He has been a capable and cheerful worker, and has carried out the difficult job of being a British Intelligence Officer to an allied Flotilla (Norwegian) well'. He adds at the end: 'good appearance' which made me smile.

What good psychologists his naval superiors were, I must say, as they seemed to have understood him very well. His most outstanding skill of course was his ability to speak different languages. This is mentioned again and again in his reports. They certainly did come in useful in the war and this is where he outshone his colleagues and possibly made up for lack in any other field.

After his time on HMS *Wells*, he briefly joined HMS *Lancaster* where he was for a short while the correspondence officer, control officer and information officer. Regarding his position as an information officer, the captain wrote, 'He takes a deep interest in current affairs and is fairly widely read in politics'. No doubt my father far preferred being an information officer to a correspondence officer where in one of his reports the captain said he had lost some keys!

He then went from ship to shore, as in October 1944 his naval records show that he was drafted to *'President'*, a shore-based establishment of the Admiralty where he worked for the director of naval intelligence. His work there was described as 'intelligence duties' which no doubt he enjoyed. After working for the DNI he was sent to Orkney on 1 March 1945 with HMS *Proserpine*, another shore-based establishment but at the R.N. Base for the Atlantic in Lyness, Orkney, used by Scapa Flow. This time he was involved in 'disarmament duties' as by now the Allies had nearly won the war.

COURTENAY AND VE DAY
8 May 1945, Orkney

VE Day, 8 May 1945 which marked the surrender of Germany, found Courtenay in the Orkneys. I asked him if he celebrated and he said he didn't really as although he was pleased the war in Europe was over, the war with Japan was not and the atom bomb was still to come. In a letter to his sister from the Royal Navy base in Lyness dated 13 May 1945, he refers to VE Day and says:

> 'Your remarks about VE day celebrations and the way it affected various people correspond very much to the incidents that took place up here. There were hundreds and hundreds of drunkards reeling about the place from lunch time to well on into the next morning. Service cars were swiped and taken for joy rides and then trashed and left in a damaged state. We were all privileged to "splice the main brace" (naval order to issue crew with alcohol) whereby all and sundry including officers were allowed to have an extra free tot of rum on the navy. All the ships in harbour sounded their sirens at midnight and really the noise was tremendous for a place which is normally so quiet.'

His time in Great Britain with the RNVR was soon to come to an end. After VE day, he had made a request to be given an appointment where his knowledge of Norwegian would be used and he finally got it. He would be sent to work with the Admiralty in Oslo. While waiting for this transfer he was based briefly in Rosyth, Scotland, with HMS *Odyssey* and worked as assistant to the Staff Disarmament Officer. The only reference to his time with *Odyssey* which in the records appears as the 'Odyssey Naval Party 1736' comes from Lt. Colonel Cairncross's report on his work when he writes: 'A very able young officer who has worked hard. Thoroughly reliable and conscientious. His command of German and Norwegian has made his services extremely helpful'.

THE LIBERATION OF NORWAY. A YEAR AND A HALF IN THE COUNTRY HELPING IT BACK ON ITS FEET.
1945 - 1946

In October 1945 he left Rosyth and sailed to Oslo. He was drafted to HMS *President* (offshore establishment belonging to the Admiralty) in Oslo as staff disarmament officer. He was to stay in Norway until April 1946.

Courtenay Lloyd participated in the liberation of Norway for which he earned the 'Liberty Medal' (Haakon VIIs Frihetsmedalje) from the king of Norway, King Haakon VII, for 'outstanding services in connection with the liberation of Norway'.

HENBURY HONOUR

It is officially announced that the King of Norway has conferred the Haakon VII Frihetsmedalje on Lt. Courtenay Lloyd R.N.V.R., "for outstanding services in connection with the liberation of Norway." The recipient, who is an Old Clifftonian, is a son of Rev. and Mrs. J. C. Lloyd, Henbury Vicarage.

AN OLD CLIPPING FROM A LOCAL BRISTOL PAPER REPORTING ON THE FREEDOM MEDAL AWARDED TO LT. COURTENAY LLOYD.

When his maternal grandmother heard about the medal, she thought he was an admiral. After all he did work for the British Admiralty. It was a joke in the family during and after the war.

When asked to elaborate why he was given the medal he modestly replied, 'Well the King had lots of medals to give out and I was in Norway so I got one...' On the occasion of his hundredth birthday, King Haakon's grandson, King Harald V of Norway, sent him a birthday card which was the biggest surprise I prepared for him for his centenary.

Without knowing it at the time, my father was part of Operation Doomsday based in Scotland. The Special Air Service Brigade landed in Stavanger from where it would advance to Kristiansand. This was an important port the Royal Navy had to sweep for mines. In 1945, after the liberation, Courtenay spent a year and a half in Oslo with the British Admiralty as part of the Allied Liberation Forces under General Thorne. As a liaison officer between the British and Norwegian navies and speaking Norwegian he was an important recruit. They were tasked with supervising the surrender of the German forces in Norway, restoring law and order, and generally helping the country back on its feet.

In a letter to Gloria dated 17 June 1945, shortly after he went out to Oslo, he describes his job as working for naval disarmament. He mentions that the letter he is writing is being typed on a surrendered German typewriter and hence there is justification for errors as the letters on the keyboard are differently positioned.

Ever interested in living conditions, lodging and food, he talks extensively in his letters about these subjects. In this particular letter he says:

'We, i.e. the officers of all services and allied nationalities are billeted in hotels. The one I am staying at is a fairly modern one with pretty good conveniences. The food, when I first came was supplied by the army and was no more than the standard 'compo' ration. This meant bully beef and watery soup for all meals except breakfast when we used to have tinned sausages and salmon fish cakes. Still I am jolly glad to say that the situation has improved considerably. In fact we are even getting fresh vegetables and beef steaks, though the latter are rather on the tough side. The Germans left behind enormous stocks of French brandy and champagne. We can, or rather could buy the stuff for four shillings (bottle of champagne) and fourteen for a bottle of brandy. Of course they looted these enormous stocks from France throughout the occupation. As you know in England such stuff runs in the region of two to five quid for a bottle and then probably only obtainable from black market sources. At the moment I have been only able to procure one bottle of champagne as I arrived here rather late on the scenes but I hope to get a few more before departing. I must say champagne is grossly overrated stuff, rather like a slightly superior cider, if that'.

Referring to how the local population lives, he tells Gloria that food for the civilian population is the same as in most other ex-occupied countries, 'rather a pressing problem.' Later he would write and tell her how it had improved. Lots of things seemed to be requisitioned from the Germans during the occupation and he mentions that the cars were mostly captured German ones.

In a later letter to Gloria dated 29 August 1945, he describes the situation in the country, including the black market again, food and the fleeing of the Nazi troops. He thanks her for her darning tips but says:

'Sorry it's too much for me. However, I have managed to persuade the cloakroom girl to do them for me. Payment will be in cigarettes. They are desperately short of them here. Such things fetch fantastic prices on the Black Market.'

He goes on to describe the food situation,

'Food situation has improved no end for civilians. In fact in most places Allied troops are allowed to eat in Norwegian restaurants. Out in the country the situation is even more favourable. In the Oslo area, i.e. within a radius of 60 miles of the city there are numerous farms which I am sure, but for the lack of transport, could more than supply the whole of Oslo area. I myself have been out in the country quite a lot of late and have been able to see things like milk and eggs without the slightest difficulty.'

He adds about his stay in Norway,

'I have requested to stay as long as possible because I know if I left here there would bound to be an appointment for me in Germany or possibly the Far East. In Germany the food situation plus starving population and all round destruction does not hold pleasant prospects.'

In the same letter he talks about his work and says,

'Of course there is still a lot of work to be done here. Although the Germans are leaving the country in large numbers each day, there is an enormous minesweeping programme still to be fulfilled and no end of ammunition to be dumped at sea.' He then describes the danger of life in Norway in those times: 'As I expect you know there was a tremendous explosion here the other day when about 40 Germans were killed, about 15 Norwegians and about 3 British or Americans. It shook the building in which I was sitting most severely and one or two windows were broken. I thought for a minute we were back in the blitzes.'

In another letter towards the end of his stay in Norway and dated 19 February 1946 he tells her he is going to Hamburg to attend an important meeting concerning the future of the German Minesweeping Organisation. About the trip he tells her

'I am travelling by rail to Copenhagen (hoping to have a day there - lashings of all kinds of food and marvelous entertainment) and then fly on to Hamburg.'

He mentions skiing there too, saying,

'Skiing is the main recreation here at the moment and I am putting in as much time at it as I can. I'm afraid progress is very slow and one gets very depressed when kids of 12 and 14 or so can do almost anything on skis including jumping 90 feet in the air - it's absolutely incredible to watch.'

My father skied in Norway but never again afterwards. He told me he learned cross country skiing. That must have been thrilling.

It was during this year and a half that he perfected the Norwegian he had begun to learn as liaison officer on board HMS *Mansfield* and he now fell in love with the country. In Oslo he met his first girlfriend, Mosse Vang at a reception held by the Admiralty. Whenever we ask him about her he blushes. I once witnessed a Norwegian citizen speak to my father in Norwegian. He later told me that he spoke it like a native. No doubt it helped that he had a Norwegian girlfriend!

His knowledge of Norway is outstanding. When he can't sleep, even today, with his amazing memory, he dozes off by naming rivers and lakes in Norway from A to Z. He has been back many times and one of his last solo trips was to Oslo when he was about 95!

My father's time in Oslo ended in April 1946. His superior, Captain Black wrote of his work there: 'A capable and reliable young officer who has done some useful work in Norway. He has a very pleasant personality, is tactful and has much common sense. He speaks Norwegian and German fluently and is quite good at Danish'. From Norway he would be sent to war-torn Germany.

IN NORWAY AFTER THE WAR.

Below is a copy of one of Courtenay Lloyd's personal files from his war records which were kindly provided by the Royal Navy Command in Portsmouth. This document is a log of all his appointments during and after the war, from training to be an officer on board HMS *King Arthur* to his missions in Oslo.

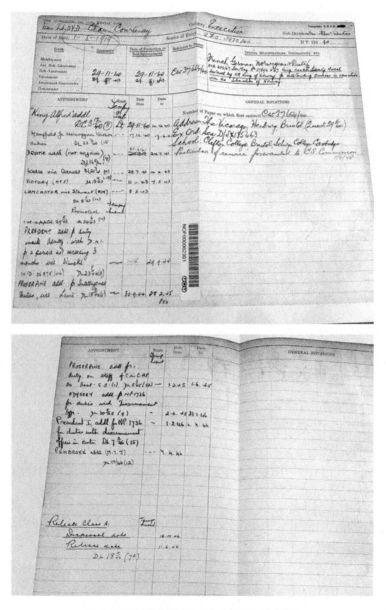

COURTENAY LLOYD'S WAR SERVICE LOG.

INTELLIGENCE OFFICER WITH THE ALLIED CONTROL COMMISSION IN GERMANY AFTER THE WAR, INVOLVEMENT IN THE RESTORATION OF ORDER, THE DISMANTLING OF THE NAZI REGIME AND CATCHING OF WAR CRIMINALS.

July 1946 to March 1948.

In 1946 the Allied Liberation Forces handed back the government of the country to Norway and thus ended his time in Oslo. Courtenay further postponed his studies when he was offered a job with the Allied Control Commission in Germany, an offer he couldn't resist. He joined as an intelligence officer and was stationed in Schleswig-Holstein in the British occupied zone. He would prove useful as he spoke German.

The Allied Control Commission was set up by the Allies to govern Germany after its capitulation. Thus Germany was divided into four areas under Great Britain, Russia, France and the USA. The main objectives of the Allies were the demilitarization of the Third Reich, the dismantling of the legacy of the Nazi regime and the restoration of order until control was handed back to Germany.

Engaged in such sensitive intelligence work Courtenay never spoke much about his assignments, always downplaying his role in the catching of Nazi criminals.

What I do know is that while in Flensburg, he was head of a small team of six whose job it was to find the criminals and hand them over to the authorities. He recruited three people from England for this job. They were German Jews who had escaped to England during the Holocaust and who took the job as they were interested in tracking down the Nazis from a regime that had been responsible for the deaths of their family members in concentration camps. He remembers the names of two of these recruits who had anglicized their surnames to Osborne and McKay. His immediate boss was another German Jew, Peter Domesen, whose original surname was Domeisen. They called him Mr. Cathedral as 'dom' in German means 'cathedral'. He knows for a fact that this man was part of the 'kindertransport' that saved many Jewish children, separating them from their families and bringing them to safety to England at the beginning of the war. I asked my father exactly how they caught the war criminals. He says this was often possible as a lot of Nazis denounced other Nazis in order to get on the right side of the Allies. He added that many of them were motivated to do so because of the Control Commission's propaganda. However, according to him, the large majority were actually hunted down by the German police who, on the one side did so as a safety net for themselves but also because they wanted to cooperate. My father is of the opinion that this was because in general most of the German population wanted rid of the Nazi legacy now that the country had lost the war. He explained to me that once the war criminals were caught, they were handed over to the British and American authorities, imprisoned and then tried, many of them in Nuremburg.

His other job was to find out what the new communist party was up to but he was also charged with helping set up a political party for future elections and the restoring of democracy. Looking back on his time with the Control Commission he says, 'It was a fantastic job. I was in the British Control Commission in north Germany for nearly two years and I always look upon that as the most interesting time I've ever had. I mean Bradford Grammar School was a rewarding career and there were terribly nice people. There was job satisfaction in one way but nothing quite as interesting as when working as an intelligence officer in Germany after the war.'

It is interesting to read about his life in Germany in those times through some of the letters in his correspondence to his sister Gloria. In a letter with an intriguing address (117 Intelligence Team B.A.O.R (British Army of the Rhine) and dated 16 March 1947, he describes the severe snow and the obstruction it caused to the population.

'For well over a fortnight now we have had terrific snow storms plus gales which have made massive drifts. The consequence is that the whole area has been completely cut off. The only thing that has been able to get through to the outside world has been one of these half-trucks or half-tracks as they call them … These have been used to get everything like coal, food etc. Towards the end of last week things seemed to take a better turn and so the mechanic and I ventured on a trip to Flensburg in the Jeep. Only a jeep could have made it. That's just the sort of vehicle I'd like to own privately, but unfortunately in England the only sort of people who can have such things are gentlemen like Lord Louis Mountbatten!'

In another letter he mentions Flensburg and asks his sister not to tell anyone as intelligence officers are not supposed to divulge their place of abode.

In many of his letters to Gloria during the war, his time in Oslo and in Germany he talks about shortages. In a letter dated 7 December 1946 from Germany, he tells his sister:

'A chap I know who is going on leave next week is taking a parcel for me containing 4 pairs of silk stockings, handbag and 2 pipes (his father smoked a pipe). I'm hoping Mum has received three food parcels I sent from Denmark.'

No doubt these parcels were very welcome in England what with rationing during and after the war.

In the same letter Courtenay describes his job a little:

'As usual I am very busy in this very interesting job of mine. To give you an idea - every Thursday evening at the Intelligence Officers' mess in Flensburg, there is a social evening to which all the local German politicians and leading lights of the Danish Minority are invited. It is most entertaining to watch how for a brief spell the politicians sink their differences and hungrily scoff the masses of corned beef sandwiches and 'poisonous' German gin that is set before them.'

He describes conditions in Germany saying

'According to the newspapers things don't seem to be improving in the UK. So really, I'm glad I'm out here, though of course really conditions are frantically bad. Black marketeering knows no bounds and competition among German officials is universal.'

He also talks about transport and here I learned that although he never drove in England or had a car, it was during his time with the Control Commission that he learned to drive:

'I've not been able to have my driving lessons for ages largely because I've never had the time. In this Intelligence Team we have one jeep which has just been reconditioned and runs like a bird. I like it because you always get plenty of fresh air. Then we have a Fordson 15 cwt for getting rations etc. and two of these Volkswagens - you know the people's car things. Luckily we never have any transport difficulties owing to the excellence of our mechanics.'

In a letter dated 2 December 1947, Courtenay tells Gloria he is getting a bit tired of his job in Germany and why. Talking about his upcoming leave in England he says:

'I will also use leave to sound the possibility of a new job somewhere because I'm getting fed up with the Control Commission. It's still interesting with bags to do but the atmosphere is a bit artificial or strange or whatever you like to call it. Although my job brings me into contact with all types of Germans day in day out, one can't forget that they are a conquered country who committed most frightful deeds, etc. during the Nazi period and in the main there has obviously been no fundamental change in their outlook.'

III

BACK TO CAMBRIDGE
1948 - 1950

GRADUATING IN GERMAN AND NORWEGIAN

Eventually my father returned to England to resume his degree at Cambridge. He changed to German and Norwegian after spending time in each country, graduating in modern languages with a distinction in Norwegian in 1950 and awarded with a 2:1. He got an MA in 1953. There were only three students studying Norwegian at the time and today it is no longer taught. He remembers his Norwegian lecturer, Mr. Ronald Popperwell and his German lecturer Mr. Foster. What a memory he has! He still subscribes to The Selwyn College magazine. Quirk of quirks is that a former pupil of Bradford Grammar School, Roger Mosey, who went on to be head of BBC TV News, is today the Master of his old college.

According to the college records, Courtenay Lloyd is the oldest living 'Selwynite' to date and the staff told me this was 'quite something to celebrate'. I totally agreed.

My father told me recently that while at Cambridge in 1950, he got a sudden windfall; £10,000 which was probably quite a fortune at the time. He said, 'Imagine, I was a student and I suddenly had all that money'. It came from an unexpected source. The family had a friend called Aunty Emily who wasn't an aunt at all. She was a very wealthy lady and my father remembers her visiting the family when they lived at the vicarage in Sledmere. Well, Aunty Emily left a lot of money to his father when she died. Out of this sudden inheritance, his father gave him and his sister Gloria part of it. If he gave them £10,000 each he must have inherited an awful lot. When I asked him what he spent it on he doesn't remember. I suggested that part of the money may have gone towards buying a house in Cambridge and he nodded in agreement. Lucky him.

MY FATHER BACK AT CAMBRIDGE. LATE 1940s

LEARNING RUSSIAN AT CAMBRIDGE
UNDER DAME ELIZABETH HILL
1950 – 1951

After graduation, Courtenay, inspired by the tales of fellow students, took a one-year crash course in Russian under the instruction of Dame Elizabeth Hill. This was his first introduction to the culture and language and he wouldn't just be adding another language to the list of those already spoken. Little did he know at the time what an influence this remarkable woman would have on his career or that the choice he made would change his life forever. He was about to become an expert on nearly everything Russian and would even marry a Russian lady.

Dame Elizabeth Hill was the first Professor of Slavonic Studies at Cambridge University. Her real name was Elizaveta Fyodorovna Hill and she was a colourful Russian-born British linguist. Her biography makes fascinating reading; *In the Mind's Eye: The Memoirs of Dame Elizabeth Hill*.

Professor Elizabeth Hill became a Dame in 1976. She was born in St Petersburg to a German- speaking Russian aristocrat mother and British businessman father. In 1917 they fled the Russian Revolution to England. It is said that Lisa celebrated her seventeenth birthday on the ship that carried the family home. Once in London the family found themselves penniless and destitute.

She gained a first-class degree in Russian at University College London in 1924, then a PhD in 1928. In 1936 she became lecturer in Slavonic Studies at Cambridge University and later professor. She was well known by everyone in Cambridge.

During the war she was a Slavonic specialist for the Ministry of Information and taught military recruits the Russian language. It is said she was a terribly demanding language teacher. This would come in useful when she was once again recruited by the government for similar purposes after the war.

Everyone in Cambridge knew her. She would apparently roar around the ancient town in her old Renault car frightening everyone. According to A.D.P Briggs in his obituary of Lisa in *The Independent* written on 6 January 1997, 'Hill's car was reputed to be the only one ever allowed to park regularly in front of the British Museum, such was her bamboozling Russian charm over British policemen.'

I heard from my father that she would often turn up at my parents' house and start changing the furniture around. Her energy was boundless. I was to meet her for the first time as an adult. It was in Norwich when she came to attend Aunty Masha's wedding with an unsuitable Englishman, Denton Burkinshaw. When she saw Denton's daughter Delia, she told my parents, 'You must hide her!' Her actual words were 'hide her in a cupboard'. I gave up my room for her at the university residence and later she told me she had spent the night reading my books on Spanish history! She was indeed a character. My parents were privileged to know her and my father owes his career to her.

IV

TEACHING
AND FAMILY
1951 - 1983

TEACHING SPIES WITH THE JOINT SERVICES SCHOOL FOR LINGUISTS
1951 - 1960

Known universally as 'Lisa', she was charged by the British Government with setting up the Cambridge branch of the Joint Services School for Linguists (JSSL), founded in 1951 and dubbed 'the spy school' by the Russians. The courses are well documented in the book: *Secret Classrooms: An Untold Story of the Cold War*, by Geoffrey Elliott and Harold Shukman, pupils on the courses. 'The purpose of these classes was to produce linguists and interpreters of Russian for military and intelligence purposes,' aka spying. The truth is that only some of them went on to be spies but we will never know how many of the 5,000 national servicemen who attended the courses actually did. My father was perfectly aware that the courses were set up for political and military reasons. He remembers there were quite a few military people around. He knew very well that he was teaching linguists to become interpreters, intelligence and signals intelligence people working for the British Government during the cold war. However, as everything was very secretive he never knew which of his pupils were actually spies or potential spies. He thinks Lisa Hill probably did. What we do know is that the famous English-born Russian spy, Guy Burgess, was tasked with getting information on the courses for the KGB. Some of the pupils went on to teach Russian like Courtenay Lloyd and some became famous such as Alan Bennett, Dennis Potter, Michael Frayn, Jack Rosenthal and Sir Peter Hall. Tony Stokes, a pupil of Lisa's and also an instructor on the courses, became a professor of Russian at Oxford University and went on to teach some of the Bradford Grammar School pupils sent there by

COURTENAY LLOYD AND HIS WIFE ELENA VON LIEVEN
IN 1955 AT A WEDDING IN CAMBRIDGE WITH LISA HILL
(LEFT). ELENA IS WEARING THE SAME DRESS SHE WORE
AT HER OWN WEDDING IN 1953.

ON THE JSSL COURSES AT CAMBRIDGE. COURTENAY LLOYD IN THE
WHITE CLIFTON COLLEGE CRICKET JUMPER HE STILL HAS TODAY.
LISA HILL IS IN THE FRONT ROW IN THE MIDDLE.

Courtenay Lloyd. Whatever their future, they all learned Russian well and in record time and have fond memories of the courses.

When the book *Secret Classrooms* was published, my father attended the celebration or presentation of the book in the Wallace Collection in London (my mother's favourite museum when she lived as a refugee there) in November 2002. There he met many of his former colleagues and pupils.

It was difficult to find native Russian teachers at the time who were unsympathetic to the Soviet cause. So Lisa asked Courtenay Lloyd if he had a job after finishing his studies to which he replied he didn't. Thus she offered him one as a teacher with the JSSL in Cambridge at Salisbury Villas. The story goes he protested saying he didn't know enough of the language to teach it, to which she replied, 'Just be one lesson ahead of your pupils'. He took her advice and it worked. Thus began his love of the Russian language and everything Russian which has lasted till today.

To quote him in Lisa's biography, 'Where else in a teaching establishment would one have as colleagues, princes, princesses, two famous artists from the Maly Theatre, Sir Winston Churchill's interpreter (Arthur Birse), a colonel and former ADC to King Peter of Yugoslavia, a Slovak aristocrat landowner, the spokesman in England for the ATS or a former Pravda correspondent who had also been a miner in Fife?'

This is an extract about him and his wife from the book *Secret Classrooms*:

'Courtney (Sic) Lloyd, whom Liza dubbed her "right hand man", shared significant parts of the administration. Remembered as having a remarkably clear and simple way of communicating the early problems of conjugation and declensions that Russian presents to the beginner, and by Phillip Hanson (later Professor of Economics at Birmingham) for his "amazing ability to recall from one week to the next who had got exactly which grammatical construction wrong the last time round", Lloyd's Cambridge studies had been interrupted by service in the Navy during the Second World War and a spell as an intelligence officer with the Control Commission in Germany. He graduated in 1950 with a degree in German and Norwegian (part of his war service had involved liaison with the Norwegian Navy). Impressed by a friend's account of the dynamism of the Slavonic Faculty under Lisa, he took a one-year course in Russian at her encouragement and joined her team. He taught as well as managed everything from organizing the setting as well as managing everything from minor problems to being the one who entered a classroom as the lesson ended to make important announcements. A shy and gentle man prone to blushing, he figures improbably in the archives as the official in charge of discipline and of reprimanding absentees and other miscreants, though doing so must have hurt him more than it hurt them; however, anything as severe as an RTU was handled by Liza herself. Lloyd later married Princess Elena von Lieven, who took conversation classes and was also the Russian secretary of the School. She was a tall good looking young woman, remembered despite her cosmopolitan background as like the hockey captain at an English girls' school.'

MARRIES A RUSSIAN PRINCESS; ELENA VON LIEVEN.
Cambridge 1953

I quote my father here saying: 'Marrying a Russian lady is the fastest way to learn Russian'.

Dame Elizabeth Hill was instrumental in my father marrying my mother, a penniless, Russian aristocrat refugee and also became my brother George's godmother. They met on the courses and their engagement was officially announced at Lisa's birthday party in 1953. Lisa Hill had a huge influence on the life of Courtenay and his family. The last time he saw her was accidently in Madrid in the summer of 1984 at the train station. He was there to buy a train ticket and she was on her honeymoon, bussing it around Spain in her eighties. A staunch spinster she finally decided to marry her male friend of many years, Stojan Velijkovic, of Serbian aristocratic background. Unsurprisingly shortly afterwards she divorced him. She was perhaps the most eccentric and fascinating person I have ever met. Although being very different, she and her right-hand man, Courtenay, always saw eye to eye.

His wife was born Her Serene Highness Elena von Lieven, a noble title in Russian aristocracy just below that of the monarchy. 'Elena' is pronounced 'Yelena' in Russian and can be shortened to 'Lyena' which is what she was often called. My mother's background and history merit a book in themselves. In short she was born in Rome in the former Russian Embassy on 7 June 1920, soon after her family fled the Russian Revolution. Her godmother was Princess Zinaida Yusupov who the family called 'Aunty Fairy' because she was such a lovely person. Princess Yusupov was the mother of Felix Yusupov, Rasputin's killer. The Yusupovs were the richest family in Russia, even richer than the Tsar. Both the Lieven and Yusupov families were friends and relatives. The direct connection is that Elena's maternal grandmother, Olga Ribeaupierre was the first cousin of Zinaida Yusupov also a Ribeaupierre before she married.

Her father Prince Andrei Lieven (1884 - 1949) was born on one of the family estates at Zmiev on the River Donets, 20 miles south of Kharkov. His grandfather Prince Andrei Alexandrovich Lieven (1839 - 1913) was a state secretary and later Minister of State Property.

Elena's father studied at the Pazhesky Corpus (noblemen's military academy) in St Petersburg and the Demidov law school in Yaroslavl. He was a poet, musician and cartoonist and, at well over six feet tall, very imposing. In 1910 he married Sophia Stachovich.

Sophia Alexandrovna Stachovich (1886 - 1961) was the daughter of Alexander Alexandrovich Stachovich III. He married Olga Ivanova Ribeaupierre. Thus Elena's mother was descended from two notable families, the Ribeaupierres and the Stachoviches.

ELENA VON LIEVEN IN FELDKIRCH, AUSTRIA IN 1945.

The Lieven family, it is said, left together with the Yusupovs on one of the last or the last ship sent by King George V to pick up Russians fleeing the revolution. It took them to the small island of Antigoni on the Princes' Islands Archipelago belonging to Turkey. They were later reunited with my grandfather Prince Andrei Lieven. He had stayed behind to fight with the White Army against the Bolsheviks. He promised God he would become a priest if he found his family again and he did. From Turkey they went to Rome awaiting the possibility of returning to Mother Russia. They had lost all their riches which were never to be recovered. I was told my grandmother, née Sophie Stachovich, had put all her jewels and most of their money in a bank in Russia before they left. When they realized it was impossible to return, the family took exile in Bulgaria. Elena's father eventually became a priest and was ordained in 1926. He was the priest of the former Russian Embassy church in the street of Tsar Kaloyan in the middle of Sofia. He was also secretary to the bishop. Later he became the rector of the new church St. Paraskeva.

When the war came and the Russians (communists to her family) finally took control of Bulgaria, Elena fled, as did her siblings Sasha (Alexander) and Nicolai (Kolya) to Berlin. She said goodbye to her adored father in 1944 and never saw him again. He died in Sofia in 1949 under the Communist regime while she was a refugee in London. His death traumatized her as she adored him. He remained forever in her heart and eventually she came to publish his poetry and manuscripts, a promise she made to herself she would do before she died. She did see her mother again when the authorities let her out of Bulgaria in 1959 as an old woman. They met in Paris at the train station and her mother did not recognize her own daughter. Later she lived with Elena and her family until her death.

When WWII ended, Elena found herself in Feldkirch in Austria where she worked for the French Control Commission helping them with displaced people. One of her roles was to detect Soviet soldiers and send them back to Communist Russia. Many did not want to go back as they could face imprisonment so she helped them.

Once the war ended, not being able to return to Bulgaria which was communist by then, she chose to go and live in London, England, to learn the language. Elena was granted refugee status but had to work cleaning homes and hospitals for two years to earn residency and a proper work permit. This she did alongside other penniless and aristocrat refugee women from war-torn Europe. All the money she earned she sent to her family in Bulgaria who needed it because of the terrible shortages there. In order to save more money for them, she even skimped on public transport preferring to walk everywhere. She got to know the streets of London like a local. Once she obtained residency and a job permit she was recruited by the BBC for their cold war broadcasts to communist countries as an announcer for their Russian service. This was where Lisa Hill found her, a 'cultured Russian' and took her on as a language instructor and course secretary for the Joint Services School for Linguists. It was on these courses that my parents met and fell in love.

I asked my father what his impression of Elena was when he met her for the first time. He said, 'Well, someone I could go out with'. Never the romantic, I didn't get any juicy bits from him for this part of the book I'm afraid. He did admit though that their first kiss took place in the 'book room' at the JSSL courses. Well, of course it had to be in a book room, they were both book mad.

They were complete opposites in character but both intellectuals who admired each other. They were both incredibly intelligent in very different ways, my mother being much more quick-witted. Ah but he was the steadfast one, the rock upon which our family was built. However, he was not complete without her and they made an unusual but fascinating couple. They were rather odd, each in their own way; odd in that they were quite special. Perhaps more than odd, they were just unique. My father is extremely quiet and reserved, a 'slow thinker' and rather solitary as you will have read in the descriptions of him written by the various captains of his ships in the war. My mother was his antithesis in that she thought at lightning speed, was gregarious, a bit of a joker and talked non-stop. He could hardly ever get a word in edgeways but then he never was a talker. I shall never forget once when we had some guests to dinner and they were all chatting away, my father listening but silent, which is quite normal for him. There was a lull in the conversation and my mother suddenly said, 'Oh, just a moment I think Courtenay is going to say something'. That made the whole group burst into laughter, my father included, and it still makes me laugh today. He is much more a listener than a talker but when he does talk he always has something interesting to say and everyone listens. However, we shall also see that when he was in the classroom he was very much the talker and all his pupils listened to him with awe.

COURTENAY AND ELENA SHORTLY BEFORE THEY MARRIED.

So there is more than one side to him as you will learn. Imagine being brought up by parents like that and in an Anglo Russian home? It wasn't always easy and I was destined to have the most unusual childhood which has marked me for life, although I think more for good than for bad. They have made me the person I am today.

I think from his very English upbringing but with a love of languages and travel, he appreciated my mother's cosmopolitan background, as well as her cultured mind. As to their looks, my father was very good looking but had no idea he was. I never thought my mother was good looking but now I can see she was when she was young. Neither of them gave a damn about their looks or about clothes. I think my mother was delighted to have finally found her rock and an Englishman to boot. At last she could settle down. Theirs was a happy marriage or as good as it gets.

After the war, her immediate family was completely split up. Her parents, older sister Olga, a nun, and her younger sister, Masha, aged 18 at the time, stayed behind in Bulgaria although Masha would later get out. Her older brother Alexander (Sasha) went to live in Montreal where he went on to work with the CBC in the sports section, and married his Russian girlfriend from Berlin. Her name was Elena Butkevich, another Elena, and they had a son Andrei who still lives in Canada. My mother knew her well from her days in the war in Berlin and she was affectionately called, 'Lenoliouk'. Her other sister Daria (Dorothea) went to New York where she became a nun. They wouldn't meet again until they were in their sixties. Her most beloved brother, 'Kolya' (Nicolai) went to live in Paris and started a family with his Russian wife Valya née Sakhagne and adored daughter Sophie (Zuka) with whom Elena had close contact until the day she died.

Elena von Lieven was a polyglot too, speaking Russian, Bulgarian, English, French, German, Italian and latterly Spanish. She was also very cultured, had a great sense of humour, was quite intellectual and a bit bohemian too. She had no dress sense whatsoever but always managed to look aristocratic. Even though she was no longer destitute when she married and set up a family with her husband, she always lived as if war rations were still in existence, never forgetting the hunger and poverty she experienced as a refugee in the war in Germany after leaving her family behind in Bulgaria.

Courtenay and Elena were married twice, first by Courtenay Lloyd's father in Bristol at his church in Henbury and then by the Russian priest, Anthony Bloom at the Russian Orthodox Cathedral in London. Religion was important to both of them; both of them were the offspring of a priest, one Church of England and the other Russian Orthodox. However, it was never forced on my brother and me.

In January 1954 they had a Russian Orthodox wedding in London officiated by the priest Anthony Bloom. Elena had two sisters who were nuns, Olga and Daria. Her older sister, Olga, who became a mother superior tried to make Elena become a nun too. In fact, before she fled

COURTENAY AND ELENA WERE MARRIED FIRST IN HENBURY BRISTOL IN A C. OF E. WEDDING OFFICIATED BY HIS FATHER. HERE ON THEIR WEDDING DAY WITH HIS FAMILY 22ND DECEMBER 1953. ELENA HAD NO FAMILY PRESENT.

Bulgaria in 1944, she had taken her first vows to become one. During the war she probably forgot about them but when her father died she became monastic.

In order to marry Courtenay, she had to get special permission from her sister Olga to break her vows who gave it to her grudgingly. Olga's reply to Elena was this: 'As you could only remain a nun in my convent and would not last anywhere else and it is not politically possible to receive you here, I agree'. Elena was happy. She believed she hadn't a chance of going to heaven, that life was too short and everything was a sin. Relieved, she happily married Courtenay. My mother wouldn't have made a good nun. She made the right choice marrying my father.

In the Russian Orthodox wedding ceremony, crowns are placed on the bride and groom's heads, as can be seen in the grainy photo below of Courtenay and Elena.

THEIR RUSSIAN ORTHODOX WEDDING IN LONDON JANUARY 1954.

Courtenay Lloyd never told anyone he had married a princess and his wife didn't generally tell anyone she was one either. She always used to say she wasn't a princess anymore after her father was ordained, a title he had to give up when taking holy orders. However the Gotha Almanac, the directory of Europe's royalty and higher nobility, still includes all her family in the Almanach. In a way we were all a little embarrassed about her title and heritage. It was such a difficult story to tell to people in those days. Courtenay Lloyd's wife, Elena, embraced England and everything English, swore allegiance to the Queen when she finally got British citizenship and felt eternally grateful to her adopted country for taking her in after the war. My mother tried to be as English as she could after getting her British citizenship. But however much she tried she remained Russian to the core. She even took on the English version of her name, Helen, although she never really liked being called it. So no, we didn't talk much about her past. Now as I, her daughter, approach my old age, I think it is a story that should be told and have become quite proud of my heritage which is rather exotic.

COURTENAY AND ELENA WITH GEORGE AND MASHA, CAMBRIDGE 1957. COURTENAY WAS QUITE A TALL MAN AT 5ft 10in AND ELENA WAS TALL TOO, AT 5ft 9in.

First they lived in Courtenay's 'digs' and after a bit of pressure from his father, they bought a house at 291 Milton Road, Cambridge. In 1955, their son George was born, followed by me in 1957.

They were delighted with their first baby. You only have to look at the smiles on their faces while holding or bathing him in the photos which grace our sitting room. It was my father who would take him out in his pram or for walks when he was a toddler before coming home for tea. As George rushed into the house upon their return to embrace his mother he would always say: 'see Mummy, have tea, baffy, beddy'. He knew his routine well.

George was born in a hospital but I was born at home. My

COURTENAY WITH A HUGE SMILE ON HIS FACE WHILE HOLDING BABY GEORGE ON HIS LAP - CAMBRIDGE 1955.

ELENA WITH GEORGE ON HER BIKE IN CAMBRIDGE.

paternal grandmother doted on my brother. He was the apple of her eye, as had been Courtenay, her first born. But when I was born apparently she uttered 'Oh, but it's a girl' as if my mother should have had another boy the same as her. Thus, not much notice was taken of me. Apparently my father's Aunty Peggy (wife of his Uncle Tom on his father's side), seeing me a bit ignored in my cot, picked me up and said to everyone, 'Look what a lovely baby girl I have here' for which my mother was forever grateful. My grandmother doted so much on my brother she used to make me jealous. My birthday is on 8 February and his was on the 12th, yet the cake she would send us every year only arrived on his birthday. In any case, both our parents loved us dearly and there was never any distinction at home about being a boy or a girl thank goodness.

My parents' form of transport in Cambridge was the bicycle like many people in this old university town. When we were small they took us everywhere with them on their bikes, just as they would when we later moved to Lincolnshire, another flat region of England.

For Courtenay and Elena the years spent in Cambridge were the happiest years of their lives.

COURTENAY LLOYD WITH HIS FAMILY
ON A VISIT TO CAMBRIDGE IN 1961.

TEACHING RUSSIAN AT THE RAF COLLEGE CRANWELL IN LINCOLNSHIRE AND LIVING IN RUSKINGTON
1960 - 1964

When the Salisbury Villas JSSL Russian courses came to an end in 1960, Courtenay Lloyd had to find another job. The natural thing was to look for jobs teaching Russian. He found one at the RAF College in Cranwell in Lincolnshire. The family moved there in 1960 and my parents bought a large bungalow called 'Fermain' on an acre of land in a small village called Ruskington, at 62 Rectory Road.

THE HOUSE IN RUSKINGTON.

Ruskington is not so far from Sleaford. My father used go by scooter for a while to Cranwell until it broke down. Later he would cycle the six miles to Cranwell and back every day. He never took his test although he had driven in Germany when he was with the Control Commission. He told me recently that as a little girl I would wait for him to come home at night. Although I don't remember as I must have been about three, he says that when I saw his bicycle lights beam on the windows I would excitedly shout out: 'Daddy coming night!' I would then tell my mother to quickly open the door by saying, 'Ope it, ope it!' Of course I

MY FATHER WITH GEORGE AND ME HOLDING OUR
HANDS IN THE GARDEN OF OUR HOUSE
IN RUSKINGTON c. 1960.

was excited as he was my daddy coming home from work and I was dying to see him. Above is a lovely picture of him with George and me in the garden in Ruskington where he is holding our hands. It must have been good weather as we are both wearing summer clothes and I am barefoot. He, however is not. He is wearing a blazer I recognize as it was one he wore for years and years. Clothes never really mattered to him.

He felt very much at home at the RAF College. It must have been a bit like being back in the forces but as a teacher. We had lots of wing commanders and squadron leaders to dinner and I remember my mother having to go out and buy a dress at Marks and Spencer's in Lincoln as she only had one old skirt and nothing suitable to wear. My father went to many functions in the evenings at the college. One year he went to the

Christmas do. There was a raffle and he won a turkey, a whole turkey. I think it still had feathers on it and my mother had to pluck it. He was as pleased as punch but found it difficult to ride home on his bike, turkey in hand. The following year he took a rucksack to carry the turkey home, imagining he would win one again. But he never did.

In Ruskington both George and I went to school for the first time. One of my main memories of the first day was being given out a slate with a piece of chalk to learn to read and write. That was the early 1960s, not that long ago. George's first memory of school may have been about eating an orange with the skin on. My mother had given him an orange to take to school but he didn't know he had to peel it. He never liked oranges after that.

We were sent to Sunday school too. I can only imagine we were sent because of my father's upbringing. It was the thing to do at the time. The best thing about Sunday school was that my father gave us a bit of money to buy sweets afterwards.

To help pay for the house, Elena got into farming with advice from local Lincolnshire farmers and began to breed chickens, ducks, geese and pigs. Courtenay wasn't too keen on that but let Elena have her way. Meanwhile, he grew vegetables in an orchard in the garden taking great pleasure in eating home grown produce. One day he came home from work and George and I were quarrelling. He got a bit cross and said, 'I want my peace!', to which I replied from my high chair: 'But Daddy there are lots of peas and beans in the garden'. He laughed and his displeasure disappeared immediately and turned into laughter. He always did like his peace and quiet.

Being a staunch anti-communist and with her great sense of humour, Elena named two of her sows after the mistresses in the Profumo scandal, Mandy (Rice-Davies) and Christine (Keeler). The male pig she called Kruschchev to everyone's amusement.

My father, not being into pigs or poultry, had a far more intellectual idea to make money to help pay off the mortgage. He embarked on writing a book which I remember took up most of his nights. Published in 1965, it is called *First Russian Reader. To Moscow*. It was designed for use as reading material for GCE pupils in those days and is apparently a simple story of a schoolboy's visit to the Soviet Union. In the preface my father gives thanks to his Russian-born wife but doesn't mention her name. I remember her protesting saying she had worked just as hard on it as he had. What I remember is feeling rather proud of seeing my father's name on a book he had written. I didn't understand what the 'M.A'. meant and was told it was 'master of arts' from his degree at Cambridge. I was even prouder when I learned that. I still have one copy and I treasure it.

THE RUSSIAN READER MY FATHER PUBLISHED IN 1965.

Towards the end of her life, my maternal grandmother came to live with us. She had previously lived in Paris and later Montreal with other members of the family after she had been let out of Bulgaria. Always referred to as 'Babushka' she frightened me a bit as she wore black, was old and bent and didn't speak English. I was very small at the time and was even more frightened when she died and her coffin was laid out in the sitting room. A Russian orthodox priest came all the way from London to spend the whole night next to her dead body, chanting in Church Slavonic and waving incense which made me rush to the bathroom in fear and lock the door. Babushka, Sophie Lieven née Stachovitch, is buried in the cemetery in Ruskington. Of course, my mother saw to it that her grave was graced with a Russian cross.

As a family we all loved the years in Lincolnshire. My parents again went by bicycle everywhere as they had done in Cambridge. I longed for my parents to have a car. My mother did buy one once, in Ruskington, but with little encouragement from Courtenay she failed her test about seven times and after that gave up. She later gave her car, a light green Herald Triumph, to her sister Masha who eventually drove it into the ground.

My mother used to drive it on the lawn at home and later ventured out onto the streets. To do so she had to have a driver in the passenger seat with her. Thus Anya Hesquith, our neighbour and friend who was Finnish, offered her services. She would sit in the front with my mother and off we would go with her son, Jeremy, George and I to explore Lincolnshire. The Hesquiths were neighbours and Flight Lieutenant Hesquith was a teacher of German and colleague of my father's at Cranwell. My father used to point out Anya's Finnish accent when pronouncing the English 'ch'. Instead of saying 'kitchen' she would say 'kitsen'. He was only pointing that out from an interest in the language. Anya came from Karelia, an area in Finland which had been torn in two by Russia, and was very bitter towards the Soviets.

So our parents took us everywhere by bicycle. One of my first memories in life is of cycling with my father. He pointed out the pink moon and I shouted excitedly, 'Pink boony, pink boony!' Whenever I see a pink moon today I always remember that moment. On those trips I remember my father pointing out the red sky, which probably came from the 'pink boony'. He said: 'Red sky at night, shepherds' delight, red sky in the morning, shepherds' warning'. Forever after I have used this expression, always remembering him teaching it to me.

The family cycling would come to an end when we moved to hilly Yorkshire. In Bradford my father walked instead of cycling and I must say he walked nearly everywhere, hardly ever catching a bus.

ELENA WITH HER CHILDREN AND
FAMOUS PIGS IN RUSKINGTON.

MOVES TO BRADFORD IN YORKSHIRE
1964

The Russian courses at Cranwell petered out too as the cold war receded and there were fewer pupils. Courtenay Lloyd had to find another job and thus the family went to live in Yorkshire where he was hired as a teacher of French, German and Russian by Bradford Grammar School, one of England's best schools. He would stay there until retirement. Another reason for leaving Cranwell was that Elena wanted a job where she could use her intellect. She must have got tired of farming and her pigs9

AN UNORTHODOX BUT VERY INTERNATIONAL HOME

The family lived in temporary accommodation with a judge's family (Douglas Forrester-Paton of Scottish origin) who had a house in Heaton Grove near the school. The Forrester-Patons were to figure heavily in our early years in Yorkshire. Douglas's wife, Agnita, was Danish, and was a great friend of my mother's. Their children were older than us but both my father and I can still remember their rather Danish-Scottish names; Tom, Kirstin and Elspeth. Their father would help our family a lot as you will read later.

We then moved to a rented cottage in Baildon on Rowntree Road until Elena found us a house in Heaton Grove too. The family moved into a massive nineteenth century, four-floor, chalet-style mansion made of Yorkshire stone and built by German wool traders during the Industrial Revolution. It had 20 rooms but only two bathrooms, one totally unusable in the cellar and one on the same floor as the main bedrooms. The bedrooms though each had basins and what lovely basins they were, the original Victorian-style ones. Elena's idea was to fill the house with lodgers from Bradford University to pay the mortgage. And a few years later she did

6 HEATON GROVE, BRADFORD.

just that and filled the attic with various students while Courtenay had to make their breakfast and serve their tea in the dining room while the family ate in the kitchen. He even helped the language students with vocabulary lists every day and they loved him.

One of the students was Sally Dalglish. Her mother never told us that Sally had mental problems until she had a nervous breakdown. That saw us take her to the famous Menston Psychiatric hospital near Guiseley. We visited her there and even took part in a fancy dress party that was organised at Christmas. My mother commented she couldn't tell who were staff and who were patients. Sally's mother was eternally grateful for my parents' help and many times offered us the use of their charming tiny little 17th century cottage called "Nokka" in the village of Rosthwaite in the Lake District not too far from Keswick. My father loved the place and so did I. He would take my friend Amanda and I along. There was no central heating and I remember the cottage being freezing. Rosthwaite is quite near Buttermere and we would walk with my father over the beautiful but very steep Honister Pass to the lake in Buttermere. There was no public transport back and it was quite a distance on foot. Amanda and I ended up taking a taxi and my father walking back. We went back many times and always remember The Lakes with great fondness.

Our home was very unorthodox although Courtenay tried to keep standards up from his genteel English upbringing. It was forever full of 'foreign' guests from all over the world, always through Elena's connections. Our house was like the 'Tower of Babel'. Once my mother even housed a family from Czechoslovakia for free who had escaped to England after the Prague Uprising in 1968. Bradford had a large population of Poles, Ukrainians and Lativians and my mother found lots of friends in these communities, feeling at home in the company of fellow Slavs. A lot of Soviet visiting teachers at Leeds University where my mother later taught would come to see us too. Through them, we got a very clear view of what life was like in communist Russia during the cold war. One of them, I think her name was Sonya Timchenko, told my mother when they arrived home that if she liked her husband she had to warn her that she would take him from her! That was the Soviet Russian women's attitude at the time. Thankfully, my father only had eyes for his wife.

Courtenay did the cleaning, the shopping - once a day and just enough for one meal - the cooking, and invariably burned some of our meals. Those were the days before Morrison's and Asda and he would shop at Mr. Pearson's and Mr. Chaney's across the road on Manningham Lane. It was nearly always 'bangers and mash' followed by some ghastly artificial desert like Angel Delight.

Those were also the days when milk was delivered by the milk man. My father always ordered just one bottle, the gold topped one with the full cream. I remember how he would siphon off the cream to have it with his coffee. He has always been very partial to cream, preferably "lashings" – to use his words – of whipped double cream. During Wimbledon, he would always buy strawberries and cream for tea which I loved and so did he. In many ways he and I love the same sweet things. When I open a box of chocolates on a special occasion to offer him one – or more – I always know which one he is going to choose as it is the one I would go for too. Like father, like daughter. My mother, on the other hand, did not have a sweet tooth. She far preferred savoury food. However, as it was my father who always did the food shopping, he only ever bought what he liked, not what she liked. Her favourite dishes were generally those that contained rice. Thus, she loved paella and when my parents bought a house in Spain she got her revenge on him.

Elena found a temporary job as a teacher of Russian at Sheffield University, and then Bradford University, until she was hired by Leeds University where she remained until her retirement in 1985. She had to bus it there and back every day and invariably arrived home in the evening well after 'teatime', too late to make it for us. Her students adored her.

My father also did the washing. No one did the ironing, although there was an ironing board in my parents' room which I had to use when nobody would iron the one St. Joseph's white blouse I possessed. In those days, people changed shirts and blouses or even underwear only once a week. It was the same with taking a bath. My father's weekly bath was on

Sunday evenings. Courtenay wasn't very good at the laundry and often the colours ran. Once all the whites turned pink, including his underwear. That wouldn't have mattered except that afterwards my father had to play in a cricket match of pupils against teachers at Bradford Grammar School. That way the whole school got to know he wore pink underpants. I think he thought he would never live it down, poor man.

Although not born in Yorkshire, Courtenay Lloyd came to love 'God's own country' but never acquired the local accent. He always insisted his children speak English with received pronunciation or 'Queen's English' as he referred to it. He loved exploring places like Bolton Abbey and his beloved Dales. His favourite walk used to be to the top of Ilkley Moor after which he would enjoy a cup of tea and a huge piece of cake at Betty's, his favourite tea shop, preferably with lots of whipped cream and would comment on how beautiful the heather on the moor was. He used to call me his 'little moors' girl' but I only went along because I also wanted to have cake at Betty's. Only later in life did I inherit his passion for walking. His other favourite places to walk and which were nearer home were Heaton Woods and Northcliffe Park. I loved those places too.

He loved sport, was a keen cricketer and hockey player and would listen to the rugby, cricket and football while hoovering our great big Yorkshire house. He would also watch the tennis during Wimbledon religiously every year. He is also a 'news freak' and as a family we would all sit down to watch the news at 6pm and 9pm, and later *News at Ten* and even *Newsnight*.

My father never failed to read his newspapers every day as he does here in Madrid. He just has to keep up with the news. Only once in his life did he fall really ill. It was on the eve of a trip to the Dales with Amanda and me that suddenly he lay down on the divan in his study and looked really unwell. It turned out he had appendicitis and there was nothing for it but for him to be operated on. It was his first time in hospital and, having never been ill, he was very afraid. My parents did not have private health insurance and he would have had to go to the BRI (Bradford Royal Infirmary) but he was so frightened, he preferred the private hospital, the Duke of York. Even while in his hospital bed, he asked me to read out the headlines of *The Times* that day. The appendicitis turned into acute peritonitis and we were called to his bedside as the doctors thought he might die. The recovery was long but he had his books and newspapers to keep him busy until he was better and able to return to school. That was a big episode in his life.

He liked to have a cup of cocoa and a piece of toast and a biscuit as 'supper' when watching the TV if it was late. It was only after much insistence, as a teenager, that I got him to like *Coronation Street* which we used to call 'Corry'. Our favourite characters were Hilda Ogden, Ena Sharples and Minnie Caldwell. His favourite TV programmes were *Doctor Finlay's Casebook*, *Steptoe and Son*, *Dixon of Dock Green*, *Softly, Softly* and series such as *Colditz* or *The Forsyte Saga*. Two other big hits with him were *The Six Wives of Henry VIII* and *Mastermind*. He always pointed out that the presenter, Magnus Magnusson was of Icelandic origin. I also remember his favourite radio programme was *Desert Island Discs*. Sometimes I listened to it with him and we both imagined what we would take to an island. Our choices were very different. He said he would take the bible; not me.

Mealtimes were full of discussions of world events and politics was high on the agenda of topics at home.

There was also a lot of talk about the war. My brother and I were brought up on the tales of my parents' experiences in the war and post war. My mother had been imprisoned in Berlin by the Gestapo and told us all the horrible details. We also knew Polish Holocaust survivors in Bradford, people who had lost whole families in the Nazi concentration camps. As a child and teenager, I would have nightmares of the Gestapo banging on our door in the middle of the night in Bradford, such was the impact of their tales of the war. Ever since then I have been fascinated with anything to do with WW2.

My parents were both anti- communist and naturally voted Conservative. My brother, George, being a rebellious teenager was staunchly left wing. However, as he was lazy he often slept through election days and my mother did all she could for him not to wake up, lest Labour got another vote. Our years in Bradford coincided with the Margaret Thatcher years. My parents were great fans of hers until even my father got tired of her when she said, 'We shall go on and on and on...'

Who doesn't remember the miners' strikes when Margaret Thatcher wanted to reduce the power of the trade unions? That was in the mid 70s and there were blackouts at night. We had to cook on my Girl Guide camping stove! I had to do my homework and my father had to do his marking by candlelight. My father called the strikers 'blasted miners' and he detested Arthur Scargill, the President of the National Union of Miners. He and my mother would utter rude words in Russian about

him. Whenever my parents didn't want us to understand something, they would talk in Russian. Ah, but we, and especially my brother, actually understood quite a lot.

On the topic of his marking, of course he couldn't watch much television as most of his evenings were taken up with this task. When it came to exam time he was very busy. I used to help him by reading out the results of each essay or exercise in question which he would then fill into a form. I always commiserated with those who did badly as I, myself, was a terrible student.

I suppose I was a terrible student because I was going through my bolshy teenage years and would sometimes frustrate my normally well- tempered father. I think he didn't like to see me becoming a woman. I well remember him tearing up my first miniskirt just as they came into fashion which broke my heart. Well, I was 12, so I suppose his reaction was normal for a father. I used to go out on Friday nights to the 'Mucky Duck', or the Black Swan as it was actually called, the BGS school hang out, a pub near us even though I was well under age being 15 at the time and to get in you had to be 18. So, every Friday I asked him for money. One day, when I asked, he threw his wallet at me exclaiming, 'Take it all!' I have never forgotten that and Eladio and I use the term often, laughingly, when I ask him for some cash.

He also frightened off my boyfriends which I did not laugh about. Kevin Wakefield was my first boyfriend and he was at my father's school which I had not mentioned to Kevin. So imagine his face when he came to our house for the first time and my father opened the door? He looked askance and said to me, 'Why didn't you tell me your father was my teacher!' That was not a good beginning. I was smitten with Kevin but I don't think my father was.

My curfew those days was about 11 p.m. One night Kevin was escorting me home and I had the feeling he was going to tell me he wanted to break off our relationship. What really broke it off and forever was when my father caught us coming in well after curfew and shouted at us both. Kevin scuttled off and I never saw him again.

I suppose my father was a very busy man really. He had to attend to us, to the lodgers, to his lessons and his marking. On top of that he gave German and French lessons at night school. The poor man used to teach at Bingley College and Shipley College for Further Education two or three nights a week.

Amanda Leonard-Myers, my friend from St. Joseph's College (our school in Bradford) and I were inseparable and she was very much part of our lives. She had a bird's-eye view of what our household was like and my father too. She always said he and my mother made a lasting impression on her. I am happy to quote her here as her memories will help readers understand just what a different and quirky sort of household we lived in and what my father (and mother) were like, in her eyes, at the time and now seen from the perspective of maturity.

'I don't suppose I have ever said this in so many words before but your father (and your mother of course) have had a big influence on my life. As you know I had very conventional English parents and while they were a steady sort of rock for me, your parents added a richness and diversity to my life that I would not have otherwise had at that age. For me they were like second parents. And the kind of second parents who I can't ever think existed anywhere else in the universe; they were so unique as an entity.

I used to love coming to your house and staying for days at a time. I always felt totally at home. Anything went and anything was possible. Your father was just this lovely quiet presence in the house. You and I were thoughtless teenagers wrapped up in our own worlds but he was always there, unobtrusive, looking out for us but never intruding in our lives. He is so educated and cultured yet never judged us on our silly antics.

I loved his study where your mother had wickedly hung a huge portrait of Lenin on one wall frowning across at a huge portrait of Franco on the other, and all the musty smelling books, and maps and furniture. It exuded scholarship and peace just like your father did then and still does today all these years later. I will never forget the hilarity when Simon (Amanda's brother who was a pupil at Bradford Grammar School) slept there one night after a party and announced the next morning he had found a piece of old Christmas cake under the sofa. I have vivid memories of him coming through the big old door from the porch into the hall with his shopping bags full of the food he would prepare later for our tea from the shop over the road. (The same shop where you would secretly go and buy huge blocks of ice cream for us on the account ... not sure why we never twigged that he would know when the bill came in).

I loved our trips to Ingleton and the Lake District, just the three of us. He would walk for miles, we would walk for a few then order a taxi back. But he just let us be ourselves, what a precious gift had we but known at the time.

He has such a precise way of speaking and always enunciated his words so beautifully placing an emphasis onto particular syllables. Despite us being self-obsessed and hardly stopping for breath, he would actually really make me listen.

There was a photograph you had of him standing in front of the big display cabinet in the yellow living room and you gaily told me you had shown that picture to friends at school and told them he was the gardener. Although this made us shriek with laughter I remember thinking at the time that was so absurd as he had the intellect of Plato, there was no way he could be mistaken for the gardener. I think I am remembering the right book when I say I read in White Swans that Jung Chang said her parents read her Ancient Chinese poetry when she was very young which she just could not understand but that over time it transferred into her consciousness by osmosis. Whether I remember correctly or not that is how I like to think his influence got through to me - I didn't appreciate it at the time but he had a profound impact on my development. And your father was the foil to your mother's gregariousness, what an amazing couple they made. Please tell him I love him too and how important he has always been to me'.

COURTENAY'S NIECE ZUKA COMES
FROM PARIS TO LIVE WITH US
Sep 1964 - June 1966

Zuka was the only daughter of my mother's beloved brother Kolya. In 1964, in her late teens, she came from Paris to live with us to learn English and study at Bradford Technical College. She and my mother spoke in French together the whole time and they were as thick as thieves. Zuka came from a very strict home and living with us and her beloved 'Tante Helene' was like living in heaven as everything was allowed. I was about nine at the time and found my cousin from Paris very chic, glamorous and beautiful.

ZUKA, MY FATHER'S CHIC
NIECE FROM PARIS.

It was through my mother that Zuka was to find her lifetime partner, Bruce. Elena had seen an advert in the paper selling beef at a very low price. She rang and ordered the minimum quantity insisting it had to arrive at 8.15 a.m. on Monday morning, just after my father would have left for school - he couldn't know. What arrived was half a cow which had not been chopped up. That was why it was so cheap. It was all panic stations and my mother asked Zuka to find someone at college who could do a butchering job before my father returned in the afternoon. She did find someone and it turned out to be Bruce Avis who had skipped his lessons to come to our house to do the butchering, not a romantic beginning to their story. My mother took to Bruce immediately and told her niece that he 'was the one for her'.

It was at about this time that my mother embarked on redecorating the old house which had probably stayed the same since it was built, and Bruce was to play a big part in not only painting and decorating, but also laying down the carpets and getting the attic into shape for the lodgers. Zuka and I remember that a lot of the furniture and bed clothes came free from St. Luke's hospital that was closing down at the time. No worries in those days of infection. Some of the bed clothes came from beds people had died on and my father was really shocked while my mother just laughed. That's how they were but, as always, he let her have her way.

Bruce and Zuka got engaged in October 1966 and were married on 24 February 1968 and what a wedding it was. The press found out Zuka was a princess and her photo and Bruce's were all over the local newspaper, The Telegraph and Argus. I have to say she was extraordinarily beautiful and she did indeed look like a princess the day she married. I shall never forget her Orthodox wedding as I was one of the bridesmaids.

ZUKA AND BRUCE'S WEDDING
BRADFORD 1968.

COURTENAY AND ELENA'S
FIRST TRIP EVER TO RUSSIA
1967

My parents' first trip ever to Russia was in 1967. They knew all about Soviet Russia but were finally going to experience it for themselves. For both of them, with their connections to Russia and Russian, it was to be an eye-opener. My mother's main impression was being surrounded for the first time in her life by people who spoke her native tongue. I remember my father describing the Soviet air hostesses on Aeroflot. He said something like they were 'large', meaning fat, of course, and rather stern looking. His description of the food was priceless; 'hard lumps of inedible chicken'. On the way out they missed their connection in Paris so were rerouted via Warsaw and had to spend the night there. My father went for a walk in the evening to explore his surroundings when he was suddenly hustled by a prostitute. He was mortified. It was his first and last experience of being approached by one and I'm sure he is glad it never happened again. My mother thought it was hilarious and it was one of her favourite stories to tell people. My parents came back with tales of life in Soviet Russia that would make your hair stand on end. My mother gave up all her underwear and most of her clothes to the ladies who stood on duty in the corridors of their hotel, The Metropol. The job of these ladies was in fact to spy upon tourists. In those days, the only way to travel to Russia was with Intourist, the country's tourist agency, and tourists were escorted and hidden from mainstream society, much as happens in North Korea today.

AUNTY MASHA COMES TO LIVE WITH US
1969 - 1970

The house was to become even fuller, noisier and even more international and bohemian when in 1969 my penniless Aunty Masha - Elena's younger sister - arrived from Germany with her son Sasha, aged 16, with just two suitcases, and knowing quite a few languages (Russian, Bulgarian, Serbian, French and German) between them but not a word of English. Elena and her sister spoke in Russian together and everything had to be translated: into German for Sasha, and into English for George and me. Wrongly in my opinion, Elena and Courtenay did not bring us up to speak Russian!

On the one hand she was influenced by my English grandmother who was not keen on her grandchildren being brought up to speak a foreign language. She very wrongly thought it would confuse our little heads.

The main reason though was that Elena wanted us to feel English and not like refugees hankering after a 'Mother Russia' we could never go to live in.

I have always regretted not being brought up to speak Russian although I am sure if I had I would be a very different person. I can feel my Russian roots and it is very frustrating when I meet Russians and tell them my mother was Russian but that I can't speak the language. Of course I understand quite a lot but not enough for a proper conversation. Aunty Masha could speak 'all the languages in the world' but she only really spoke two perfectly; her native tongue Russian, and Bulgarian the language of the country she was brought up in. She had terrible difficulties learning English and sometimes knowing German didn't help. She kept saying 'sex' instead of 'six' which caused much hilarity. She also used her two fingers for the victory sign quite often but did it the other way round which in English is very rude. It must have been around her first Christmas with us and people kept saying, 'Merry Christmas'. She was puzzled and would say; 'Christmas, yes, how they know my name Mary?' On paper, her name, like mine was Maria, not Masha. All girls called Maria or Mary in Russian are referred to as Masha, the diminutive of Maria. She was very fond of cottage cheese but called it 'cottages'. Once she went looking for a shop to buy some and was directed to an estate agent!

My mother turned to our judge friend, Douglas Forrester-Paton who was instrumental in getting Aunty Masha residency and work permits. He even got her out of the odd scrape, for instance, when she had a car accident. It was quite a thing in those days to have a judge as a friend. My father was always embarrassed to ask him for favours, my mother never was.

Their arrival totally disrupted our household. My aunt completely monopolised my mother and both my father and I felt rather abandoned. Mealtimes were complete havoc and noisy. Sasha was four years older than I and, aged 16 naturally had a huge appetite for a boy of his age. I remember how he used to make lots of toast from loaves of "doorstop" as my father used to call the English style packets of sliced white bread. We didn't have a toaster in those days and he used the old fashioned grill on the cooker. Sasha would often burn the toast, making a lot of clatter which just added to the general noise created by us all in the kitchen. But one night at dinner, when everyone was talking loudly as usual he suddenly stood up, banged the table and nearly shouting announced, 'I am now going to tell you about my day! I got up at seven o'clock, got George off to school, walked to Bradford Grammar School …' and went on until he had finished describing his day. There was total silence in the kitchen. I think everyone got the message. They didn't stay for more than a year and life was more peaceful when they left to live in rented accommodation in a street near my school. We all loved Aunty Masha dearly but her presence was so huge she was difficult to live with.

Her background deserves a mention here as she figured heavily in our lives and in my father's marriage. As I was called Masha too, there had to be a way to distinguish between us, thus I became known in the family as 'Baby Masha'. Seven years younger than Elena they were devoted to each other although they quarrelled an awful lot, Aunty Masha usually winning the argument. On her deathbed, their mother had made Elena promise to look after her younger sister until the day she died, a promise she always kept through thick and thin.

Her Serene Highness Princess Maria von Lieven, more commonly known as 'Aunty Masha' was born in Sofia on 21 September 1927, and died in Villajoyosa (near Alicante) in Spain in 2008. She was the beloved sister of Elena, and the youngest of the six brothers and sisters: Alexander

(Sasha), Olga, Dorothea (Daria), Helene (Elena), Nicolai (Kolya) and Maria (Masha). She was vivacious, extremely beautiful, glamorous, a total adventurer, somewhat bohemian, a great saver of people in distress, a lover of life but also a very unlucky woman. She was the mother of Sasha, her only son but also of a daughter, Sophie who was born prematurely and died two weeks after her birth in Germany in the late 1960s. When she was aged just 16, Masha rushed to Yugoslavia from Bulgaria with her friend, Nina, to fight in the resistance against Marshal Tito. Later she studied forest engineering. Far more interested in the theatre, afterwards she studied drama and became an actress. She married another actor, Boris Manov who turned out to be a drunk. In 1959 she left him and fled Bulgaria for Paris after having sent Sasha ahead a year before. Her story also deserves a book. Once in England, Elena helped her find teaching jobs and she taught for a while at St. Joseph's College (my school) until she found a position in the Russian department at the University of East Anglia under Professor Tony Cross. While living in Norwich she married Denton Burkinshaw and later divorced. It was Masha Lieven who first bought a house in the small village of Bolulla, near Callosa

COURTENAY'S SISTER-IN-LAW PRINCESS MARIA VON LIEVEN, ELENA'S YOUNGEST AND MOST GLAMOROUS SISTER. PARIS 1959.

in Spain a country she came to love, and inspired Elena to buy one too. She died there in 2009 and is buried in Alfaz del Pi (Alicante).

Stories of Aunty Masha pepper this biography but there is one story in particular that stands out in my mind. If I did write a book about her it would be called *Travels with my Aunt*. Our first trip across Europe was in 1969 in one of her battered old cars, just after the first Norwich Russian course had finished and which you will read about later.

Her car was actually a van with no windows or seats in the back where my mother and I would sit or lie while my father was the co-pilot, map in hand to guide his sister-in-law to Germany. Seat belts either hadn't come in yet or weren't yet obligatory. The trip was a bit of a mystery to me.

I was 12 and my parents and aunt were taking me with them to Germany to see an old friend from Bulgaria called Lyoka. I didn't realise it at the time but my mother and aunt were really going there to get a facelift and a 'boob job' done by a German surgeon recommended to them by Lyoka.

In 1969 my mother and aunt were 49 and 42 respectively and looked fine to me. This sort of surgery was completely new in those days and was not available in England. Only my mother and aunt were crazy enough to travel abroad to do such a thing. My father went along for the ride as did I. He wasn't at all interested in his wife's or sister-in-law's operations but was always game to visit Germany or Holland.

Throughout the long journey my aunt wore the same black-and-white striped jersey dress. My father said she looked like a football fan.

I think it was at Aachen on the Dutch border with Germany where we stopped at customs. We must have looked a funny group. My aunt, being friendly and always saying the wrong thing at the wrong time, suddenly my father looked at a tree on the border and asked the border official in German whether the tree belonged to Germany or to Holland.

Suddenly the official suspected something and he searched the old van and us thoroughly. When he looked at our passports and saw that the profession on my father's was 'Schoolmaster,' the officer looked at him with more respect and also surprise, and said, 'Schulmeister!' as if he couldn't believe someone as respectable as my father could be travelling with such a group.

We have never forgotten the incident. There are many more with my aunt but too many to tell here. I keep forgetting this is my father's biography and not my mother's or my aunt's although their lives are all so entwined.

DEATH OF HIS SISTER GLORIA
AND HER FAMILY IN AN AIR CRASH
Rijeka 1971

On 23 May 1971, my father's sister Gloria, aged 44, her husband Derek, and children Jacqueline (12), Michael (9) and Anthony (7) flew out to Rijeka on holiday to visit the Isle of Krk. This island in former Yugoslavia was where Gloria and Derek had met and fallen in love and they wanted to show 'Mummy and Daddy's island' to their children. Gloria had been taking care of their mother when she died at the end of 1970. With some of the inheritance money Gloria was able to afford their first trip abroad as a family. The flight, a Russian charter plane, took off at Gatwick airport and landed in bad weather. Shortly afterwards it burst into flames.

GLORIA HIS SISTER.

There were seventy-eight people on board and only five survived. We saw news of the crash on the TV that night and my father remarked that his sister was travelling to Yugoslavia. He tried ringing her at her home in Ickenham (near Uxbridge in Middlesex) but sadly never got an answer. When he got the fatal phone call from the Gatwick Airport authorities the morning after the crash, he put the receiver down and commented to his wife, 'I only have you (the family) left now.'

This was a tragedy that has lived with us always. I cannot begin to imagine what it was like for my father to lose his beloved sister Gloria. Now he had lost both his siblings.

My father was very close to his sister Gloria. He still has all the letters they wrote to each other during the war. Born in 1926, she attended The Clergy Daughters' School in Bristol, later renamed St. Brandon's School. It seems fitting as she was the daughter of a clergyman. When war broke out she was quite young and because of the German bombing (Bristol Blitz), she and some of her fellow pupils, a small group of 11 or 12 girls were evacuated, as city children were in the war, to Wells. In Wells the girls were accommodated in different houses. My father remembers that Gloria stayed with a lady called Constance Gill and would be there until she joined the war effort herself. Apparently my grandfather told the rest of the family: 'She is in the house of Connie Gill'.

Towards the very end of the war, she joined the WRACS (Women's Royal Army Corps), first as a private and later she was promoted to corporal. Her main task during her time with the army was as a driver. Contrary to her brother Courtenay, she was an excellent and very skilled driver and, I suspect, a good mechanic.

During the war Courtenay and Gloria corresponded almost weekly. In one of his letters to her written from the Royal Naval base in the Orkneys

GLORIA, AN ARMY CORPORAL (DRIVER) IN ABOUT 1947 (ON THE RIGHT).

and dated 3 May 1945, he mentions her job with the WRACs: 'So you are going to stick it out until the end of the Jap War are you? Jolly good show'.

In another of his letters he congratulates her on being promoted from private to corporal but warns her not to become an officer. He says, 'Promise me never to become an officer, it spoils a girl - at least it does in the W.R.N.S. The feeling between officers and ratings in the W.R.N.S. is never very good anywhere. Yet there are no end of WRENS who could easily get commission but they don't because it makes them such outcasts'. Gosh, we women complain today about not being equal to men. Gloria had it far more difficult.

Here is her soldier's Service and Pay Book. It makes for interesting reading. She loved her times with the army.

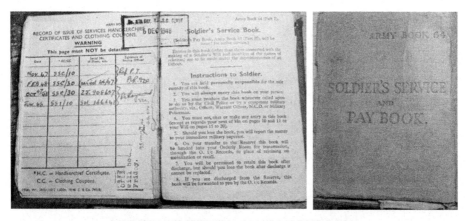

COURTENAY'S SISTER GLORIA'S SOLDIER BOOK.

For this biography, I asked my father to describe his sister Gloria. He said she was quite independent and very respectful of her family. He said she didn't have many boyfriends so maybe Derek was her first love, but we shall never know.

And so, after the war she met and fell in love with Derek Orchard. They were to meet on the Island of Krk, ironically the destination that would lead them to their death in 1971. They were married five years after Courtenay and Elena in February 1958, again at their father's church, St. Mary's, Henbury. There must be nothing more joyful for a vicar and his children than for him to officiate at their weddings.

GLORIA AND DEREK'S WEDDING AT ST. MARY'S, HENBURY, 8 FEBRUARY 1958.

Gloria got on very well with my mother and welcomed her into the family despite her 'foreign' origins for which my mother was forever grateful. According to my father, my mother called her 'posh Aunty'. She was a bit posh but in a very nice way. Once the two of them were preparing lunch for their husbands and by mistake the freshly cooked sausages fell into the coal bucket. There was no time to make anything else, so they washed them and served them without saying a word of what had happened until a long time afterwards.

Gloria and Derek set up home in the small town of Ickenham (in Middlesex but just outside London) at an address that is etched in my memory; 18 Ivy House Road. They had three lovely children, Jacqueline, just two years younger than I, Michael, and Anthony.

When Courtenay's niece Jacqueline was very small she couldn't pronounce his name and called him 'Uncle Cockin'. He has always remembered that.

Our two families were very close and we always spent Christmas with them. By then Courtenay's parents had gone to live in Ickenham too (17 Hoylake Crescent) just after my grandfather had retired in 1957, to be near Gloria. We spent lovely times together and many an evening at Gloria's house playing Monopoly together. She played the piano well, the one we now have at home which belonged to her mother and which no one plays anymore. She would take us on day trips in their car, an old

UNCLE DEREK, GLORIA'S HUSBAND
HOLDING BABY JACQUELINE, THEIR
FIRSTBORN, 1959.

Humber, to places in the vicinity such as Windsor Park, Burnham Beeches, the model village in Beaconsfield, and Black Park in Buckinghamshire adjacent to Pinewood studios. She would also take us into London to see the Christmas lights and I remember vividly being taken to see the Natural History Museum.

The only thing I remember about Derek Orchard was that he worked for an engineering company, Vickers I think, and would go to work on a Vespa, leaving the car to Gloria. I also know he was a Tottenham Hotspur's fan. He was kind to us as 'in-laws'. I first learned that expression when as a child I was sleeping on a divan in their dining room and the phone rang. He came in and picked up the phone and I heard him say, 'I have the in-laws here'. I shall never forget.

Tea at Gloria's house was very English. Contrary to my friend Amanda, at the time I didn't appreciate our international and unorthodox household and funny parents, far preferring the Englishness I craved. I found it at my Aunty Gloria's and grandparents' houses and basked in it. Even my father became more conventional when he was with his immediate family and I found it funny that they called him 'Court'. Tea always included jam sandwiches which I adored at the time. If my father was quiet, his sister was much more extrovert, as was their father who was a really jolly person to use a term of the times. I adored my Aunty Gloria.

Gloria and Derek were pillars of society in Ickenham, being active members of St. Giles Church (they are buried there), belonging to the tennis club and doing things like taking part in the 'cheese and wine' parties that were so popular at the time. I remember wishing my parents would do things like that. I was wrong of course, as my unorthodox upbringing, possibly through the osmosis Amanda mentions earlier, has made me the person I am today, neither Russian, nor English, nor Spanish, but rather a sort of person of the world.

Those family encounters were to be sorely missed and only kept in our memories. After the funeral - the church was jam packed - my father spent the whole night at Gloria's house, sitting in their living room. My heart went out to him. The news of their death was unbearable to all of us but for him it was a much bigger blow. He hardly ever spoke about her after their deaths but I know he still suffers in silence at the loss of his wonderful sister Gloria.

ONE OF THE CHILLING CLIPPINGS OF THE DEATH OF GLORIA'S CHILDREN, MY COUSINS AND MY FATHER'S NIECE AND NEPHEWS.

There was much newspaper coverage of the family's death as they were a whole family with three children. It was terrible to see them, my cousins, my father's niece and nephews' photos splashed across the front pages during the days after the crash. We only got *The Times* at home but even though my father tried to hide them from us, I did see them at the post office across the road. It's still chilling for us to look at them but I am including one here as their death is an important part of my father's biography. There are many more in a file in my father's room but it is too hurtful to go through them. The children were just 12, 9 and 7 when they died, their lives suddenly cut short. They remain in our hearts and minds and will do until the end of our days. RIP Gloria, Derek, Jacqueline, Michael and Anthony.

Astonishingly, I have Gloria's very last letter to her brother from their correspondence over the years, written the night before they left to go on holiday. I shall partially reproduce it here: 'I don't think I thanked you for your welcome letter. Enjoyed all your news. Still haven't sent you a birthday present. Will send something on return from holiday. Frantically preparing to go tomorrow. Due to take off from Gatwick 5.30pm tomorrow, arriving Krk airport 9.45pm. All in excited anticipation. Hope to see you during the summer hols. Perhaps we could pop up and see you in between Norwich and any other plans you have. Love from all to all. Gloria'. We would not see them in the summer holidays or ever again.

A HOUSE IN SPAIN AND THE 'CALLOSA DAYS' - FRANCO'S TIMES
1972 - 1984

The family would travel abroad every summer. There was no money at home for superfluous or luxury things - Courtenay and Elena were both teachers - but there was always money for travel. We mostly did so on the cheap, by train or with Elena's eccentric sister Masha in her old car. In about 1972 and inspired by her sister, Elena bought a house in Spain in a small town called Callosa de Ensarría in the province of Alicante. Aunty Masha had bought a house in a smaller village further up in the hills, called Bolulla where the villagers still refer to her as 'Señora María'. It cost her £500 and there was a donkey in the front room when she acquired it. My mother got ours for a song, just over £1,000. In those days there was a limit to the amount of sterling you could take out of the country and the only way to pay for the house was in cash. So, my mother hid the £1,000 inside a cooked chicken which she sat eating in Aunty Masha's car as they crossed the border and went through British exit customs. Our house was on a street called *Calle de las Flores* (Flower Street) number 6, I think, but there were no flowers on it. Both villages are nestled in the mountains and surrounded by orange groves, about 20 km inland from Benidorm but with not a tourist in sight. We were possibly the first English or foreign family to buy a house in the area and we were the object of much fascination in both Bolulla and Callosa. Once we were asked whether people in England believed in God! My mother used to walk on the streets barefoot.

One day a small gypsy girl came up to her and seeing her barefoot too, asked her whether she was also poor. My father loved the exoticism of being in a rural village of Franco's Spain. He would buy the local paper - you couldn't buy a national paper there in those days - *La Verdad* (The Truth) but there wasn't much truth in it or so my father said. He would go out and do the shopping there too and come back with juicy red tomatoes, fresh bread, cheese and hams which we all ate with gusto. Everything was cheap. For £1 we would get about 250 pesetas. Alcohol was dirt cheap and spirits were poured into big glasses right to the top. It was funny but alcohol cost less than Coca-Cola.

We got to know Franco's Spain which was pretty poor at the time but fascinating and exotic for us. Being keen linguists, both Elena and Courtenay learned Spanish well and it is thanks to them and my aunt that I went on to study Spanish at Nottingham University and live in Spain. But that's another story.

COURTENAY ENJOYING WALKING THE MOUNTAIN ROADS NEAR CALLOSA IN SPAIN - SUMMER 1973. (PHOTO ANDREW DALE).

My father loved the walks in the mountains. We preferred to go to the beach in Benidorm which was only a little less crowded than today. My father hated it and my mother called it the 'rubbish bin of Europe'.

There were only two buses every day, so we would often hitch-hike in the boiling sun, sometimes walking part of the way. When Aunty Masha took us by car, my father sometimes joined us. He was happy to be able to buy *The Times* and would sit on the beach fully dressed reading it and sticking out like a sore thumb among the British tourists. He far preferred walking from Callosa to Bolulla or to the lovely waterfalls at Algar on the way. He never bathed, although when he was young he did like swimming.

We would go every year until my parents sold the house, well in fact there were two to sell as my mother bought another one which my father was dead against. They sold them shortly after our marriage and some of the proceeds went to help us pay the mortgage for the house Eladio and I bought in Madrid when we married. My parents were always very generous with us. Aunty Masha never sold her house in Bolulla. It was only after her death in 2009 and many years later that her son Sasha sold it. I wish I had known and maybe we would have bought it. We all look back with nostalgia on the 'Callosa days'.

THE NORWICH RUSSIAN COURSES –
UNIVERSITY OF EAST ANGLIA
1969 to the 1990s

In those days Courtenay, Elena and Aunty Masha taught on the famous Norwich Russian courses organized by the University of East Anglia under the leadership of Professor Tony Cross every summer. The first year they were held only my mother and my aunt were hired. But in the middle of the course Elena was called away to interpret for Archbishop or Metropolitan Pitirim at the World Council of Churches conference at the University of Kent. He was another colourful feature of our life being one of the three senior bishops of the Russian Orthodox Church during the latter part of the Soviet era. My mother was very proud of being his official interpreter whenever he needed her services outside Russia. Once she went to Uppsala to interpret for him. She was paid in cash. My father hid it in one of his thousands of books in his study at home. When he went to look for it he couldn't remember in which book he had put it. One day, Sasha, my cousin looked through every single book but the money my mother earned thanks to Archbishop Pitirim was never found. When my mother had to leave Norwich for Kent, my father stepped in for her and took me with him. I was aged 12 at the time and found it all very exciting. From the following year until the courses finished in the 1990s all three of them were a permanent fixture.

Tony Cross, now Emeritus Professor of Slavonic Studies at Cambridge University where my parents' whole story began – what goes around generally comes around – learned Russian on the JSSL courses. At the time the Norwich Russian courses started he was head of the Russian department at East Anglia and would go on to be Aunty Masha's boss.

Years later he went on to be my mother's boss too when he became the Roberts Professor of Russian at the University of Leeds. He and his family were quite close to my parents. I remember once going to have lunch at their house in Ilkley, that pretty little posh town in West Yorkshire. My brother George came as did my new boyfriend Eladio. I can't remember what we ate but I do remember there was just one potato for each guest. We all looked on aghast when George helped himself to two which meant there weren't enough to go round. Ever since then, whenever there is not enough food on the table we always remember 'Doctor Cross's potato'.

The three-week summer courses were very popular with students of all levels from all around the world. It wasn't so easy to travel to Russia to study in those days which was why they were in such demand. My parents enjoyed teaching there every year, being part work and part pleasure, and my father used to call them 'a busman's holiday'. At these courses, Aunty Masha would both run and put on the course concert on the last night every year. Every year she single-handedly created a first-class Russian choir out of about a hundred unknown people, not one of whom was a professional singer. She would put on superb sketches and the actress in her would bloom and she looked magical and beautiful on the stage as the audience applauded wildly.

At the courses they made many friends from both England and abroad who would often come and visit us in Callosa afterwards. One of their pupils who came out to Callosa was Andrew Dale, the prizewinner of the courses every year he attended them. He later went on to study Russian at Oxford University. Today he works for the UN in Geneva and he remains a friend of the family. Andrew Dale has this to say about my parents which I have to include in this biography as he describes them so well.

'Your parents were very special to me. Coming from a rather oppressive home, when I came to stay with you in Callosa I delighted in discovering a family where fun was the basic principle, the wonderful sense of freedom and joy of living that you all communicated, their originality, erudition, knowledge, and the pleasure with which they shared everything. They were probably the most generous, entertaining, and welcoming people I have ever known.

I learnt so much from them. At Norwich I looked forward to their lessons with joy: Courtenay was an inspired teacher, full of unforgettable examples of word usage and going off at unforgettable tangents, Elena a constant entertainer with her colourful anecdotes, her great sense of fun and humour, and love of word play. Tell Courtenay I think of him often and will never forget their encouragement and help. I feel very privileged to have known them'.

We remember Andy's visit very well. He was extremely intelligent but also extremely shy at the time and maybe we seemed overbearing. He was also only used to English food which would prove a problem in Spain. I remember he ate melon for the first time in Callosa. Desperate he wouldn't eat anything, my mother took him to the little supermarket in Bolulla to see if anything would take his fancy but of course the produce on offer was very different to a supermarket in England. Today he is a changed man, very cosmopolitan and international. So, no wonder, that visit to Callosa must have had a big impact on him.

Tony Cross and his family also bought a house in Bolulla as did his University of East Anglia and Norwich Russian Courses secretary, the lovely and vivacious Beryl Ranwell with her husband Derek, a botanist. While writing this biography, Andrew Dale told me that Beryl had gone on to be the secretary to the famous German author W. G. Max Sebald who died tragically in 2003. Slowly Bolulla became full of Aunty Masha's assorted international friends some of whom are still there today.

COURTENAY AND ELENA AT THE NORWICH
RUSSIAN COURSE IN 1990.

HIS TIME AT BRADFORD
GRAMMAR SCHOOL
1964 - 1983

In 1964 my father joined the Modern Languages department as Senior Russian master and teacher of French and German first under GNC (Nicky) Nicholls and later under Harry Davis. Nicky Nicholls' son, Steve, also his former pupil, reminded me that our parents were friends, especially his mother Helen and my mother. His sister, Claire, remembers playing at our house in the 60s. Courtenay Lloyd preferred teaching German and Russian to French mostly because he had to teach French to younger, less interested and more unruly pupils. He far preferred his A level Russian classes where his pupils had chosen to study the language. He also offered both a Scandinavian and Eastern European option in the 6th form, something I learned from his old boys. His former pupil, Mike Wilkinson, remembers also a trip to Denmark organized by my father in April 1966. The headmaster at the time was Kenneth Robinson who lived at the lovely Clock House, later the younger boys' school.

I am sure that no one at Bradford Grammar School could imagine that their teacher or fellow master lived in such an unorthodox and international household although a few of them did come to his house. I went to St. Joseph's College next door and many of my friends and boyfriends came from BGS. Having generally very permissive parents, I held many a party at our enormous house and my father would hide when any of his pupils were there, bless him. However, he was once caught out by some of them who saw him frying chips and wearing an apron! Simon Leonard, my friend Amanda's brother, stayed the night with us once and slept on the divan in my father's study. While making

Courtenay Lloyd

1964−83

THE PHOTO OF COURTENAY LLOYD IN THE MASTERS' CORRIDOR AT BGS.
IT'S NOT ONE I LIKE AS HE LOOKS TOO SEVERE.

up the divan, Simon found a piece of old Christmas cake my father had hoarded under the bed and obviously forgotten about. Simon though has never forgotten the incident. and which his sister Amanda records in her tribute to my parents earlier in this book. Courtenay always used to hoard chocolates and sweets, mostly so neither George nor I would find them. As I say elsewhere, he has a very sweet tooth which I have inherited. But lucky him, he can eat what he wants; chocolate, cakes, the lot and never gets fat. He obviously has incredible genes.

BRADFORD GRAMMAR SCHOOL IS A VERY IMPOSING AND BEAUTIFUL BUILDING.

After his morning household tasks, my father would walk to school and then back past Lister Park every day. Sometimes he had to do 'bus stop duty' which he hated. My father did not like having to mete out discipline yet his pupils respected him always. One of them, Daniel Livingstone, told me that he put the fear of God into them in the first lesson and from then on was the perfect gentleman, gaining their complete respect. He was a form master, and housemaster of Lister House as well as head of the Railway Society. The latter he enjoyed enormously and many a trip was organized to the National Rail Museum in York or on the Settle Carlisle railway.

He also had to do his share of detention supervision, something he disliked. In one of his weekly letters to me when I was at Nottingham University he said, 'I am writing to you in the most dreary and uncomfortable classroom in the school while supervising detention for such misdemeanours as smoking in the toilet (8 culprits), repeated failure to hand in work on time, laziness, calling out, persistent giggling, pulling another boy's hair, not attending assembly. So you can see how much I am enjoying my so-called "feet up" afternoon. If I really had time off and there were no chores then I would be reading some Spanish or Russian book'. As regards marking, in the same letter he writes: 'I have a most desperately boring set of French exercise books in front of me which I shall have to start marking sooner or later'.

The teachers in those days were called 'masters' and wore flowing black graduate gowns. Some pupils told me his was always full of chalk! Many of the masters had nicknames and Courtenay Lloyd's was 'Clarence'. No one has ever been able to give an explanation as to why. Was it because of Clarence the Lion or his initials, I wonder?

Courtenay was a quiet and shy man at home, his wife being the heart and soul of the family. But he obviously came into his own at school, especially in his Russian lessons. Many a former pupil has written to him to say what an impression and influence he had on their careers. They also describe a man totally different to the father I knew at home. In his classrooms, especially teaching Russian, he showed his true self and became passionate about his task and was a sort of showman in the eyes of many of his pupils. He was so passionate about teaching Russian that he went way beyond his responsibilities of sticking to the grammar and text books, and gave his pupils a proper glimpse of what life was like in the Soviet Union at that time.

Russia in the 60s and 70s was very much a forbidden country but he managed to take a group of pupils to Moscow and Leningrad

(now St. Petersburg) one year which was to coincide with New Year's Eve, where his pupils could witness and experience his teachings at first hand.

They have never forgotten that trip.

His closest colleagues were Harry Davis, head of the Modern Languages department, Roderick Thomson, teacher of English who was known as "Roddy" to his pupils Raymond Shaw Smith who taught Classics. Raymond had a farm out in the Dales and we once went to visit. I remember my mother telling me about a dinner at the Davis' who lived in Shipley. My father, who is a very fussy eater, a bit like me, hates liver and always has done. At the dinner that night, it was liver that was served. My mother was sure my father wouldn't touch it. However, his politeness took over and not wanting to embarrass his hosts, he didn't protest and managed to eat it. He was then served seconds which he could well have refused. Again, his politeness rose to the fore and he accepted seconds. I felt very sorry for him. As you can see, politeness always came first for him and he would rather have died than made his hosts feel uncomfortable.

They also visited us in Callosa.

He also fondly remembers the Head of Studies, another teacher of French, H. A. Twelves, whose nickname was 'Douzie'. My father used to tell us that Mr. Twelves was a Christian Scientist and because of his beliefs could not receive medical care. That worried me a lot at the time. He was, according to all reports, a formidable Head of Studies and teacher.

Funnily enough he and another teacher, Freddie Somers (known to the pupils as 'Charlie'), were both Selwyn College Cambridge graduates. When asked about the headmaster Kenneth Robinson, he said he was a distinguished man and much appreciated.

When asked to recall the names of outstanding pupils or those he remembered most he includes in this order: John Asquith, David Whitlam, Simon Hewitt and John Starkey. He also got to know two other ex-pupils very well, Andy Myers and Simon Leonard, through my best friend from St. Joseph's College, Amanda née Leonard who is Simon's brother and Andy's wife. Courtenay was Simon's housemaster and Andy's form master. They have been to Madrid to visit and the three of them talked fondly of their times at BGS. I'm not sure if this is the right place to mention it but it was in our house and at one of my parties that Andy and Amanda first fell in love.

NOT SUCH A SAINT.
MY FATHER, ACCORDING TO
SOME OF HIS PUPILS

If you have got this far into his biography, by now you are probably thinking my father is a bit of a saint. Well, no he wasn't I can assure you, although he is now he is in his old age. Throughout this biography I have painted my father as a quiet and gentle man. This he was for me most of the time. He hardly ever got a temper but when he did, all hell broke loose, and I as a teenager, was often on the receiving end of it. Some of his pupils were too.

One of them, Julian Michael Kiely, recently said this about his teacher Courtenay (and although it may not be politically correct to include here it is hilarious so I will do so): 'He was a great teacher. Not afraid of using unconventional tactics, such as calling me a 'filthy idle swine' which is probably about right".' I was shocked and asked what had provoked my father to utter such words from his gentlemanly mouth. Julian explained, 'I rashly admitted I probably performed best with a boot up my backside. He did look a bit self-conscious about delivering said boot'. I replied, laughingly, that he had deserved the words my father delivered.

Julian told me that Simon Hewitt, one of my father's most illustrious pupils, 'used to keep copious notes on Clarence's most deathless utterances' and wondered if he still had them. I knew about them because Simon had sent me a copy a few years ago. They are priceless and I am including them in this biography (Appendix VI) so that the full picture of him as a teacher can be recorded properly. I am eternally thankful to Simon for his note taking during his teacher's lessons! Simon, who lives in Switzerland, came out to see my father in Madrid in 2016 and it was a most lovely reunion.

COURTENAY AND SIMON HEWITT IN MADRID, APRIL 2016.
TEACHER AND PUPIL REUNITED 40 YEARS ON.

I asked Simon whether he had written them as a pupil, something I found quite surprising for a teenager, and he had. He replied, 'Journalistic instinct I guess, Masha - and nothing surreptitious about it.' He went on to explain that my father even knew about it. 'To begin with I think your father thought I was taking extra-conscientious notes, but he soon realized he was being recorded for posterity and threw me sideways glances after his colourful comments, of which there were about ten a lesson'. These are just some, the rest can be found in the full transcript in Appendix VI.

'We'll just have to soldier on' he would exclaim motivationally. 'We must hold out, stick it out, and finish the book. That's the great thing!'

This was his catchphrase:

'Fibberty-gibbet is my type of word!' he assured us proudly. 'It's got panache, that's the great thing!'

It is difficult for me to write more about his times at Bradford Grammar School as I was not there to witness him. He is much better described by some of his 'old boys', now in their fifties and sixties who have reached out to me over the years via my blog (www.mashalloyd. blogspot.com) or on social media to tell me just how much influence my father had on them. From these emails and messages I have discovered just what a unique teacher he was. Being the modest man he is I think he had no idea just what an inspiring teacher he was and how much he influenced the lives of his pupils, all of whom went on to have great or even glittering careers.

Here are just a few extracts from some of their messages with their feelings and memories. The full quotes can also be found in Appendix VI.

Jonathan Starkey says, 'There are so many of us spread across the globe who owe much to Mr. Lloyd's teaching qualities and inspiration'.

David Whitlam, ex-head boy, told me my father taught him Norwegian when he was 12 and later prepped him for Swedish O level which was not part of the school curriculum during the lunch hour. He called my father 'the greatest influence on my whole academic life' and added, 'I owe this amazing man so much. Courtenay Lloyd, my Russian, French and Swedish teacher at Bradford Grammar School. You advised me to go to University College, Oxford for Russian in 1978. You will be 100 years old this year. You made my life'.

John Asquith is grateful to his old teacher for lending him records of Russian operas and choral music, thus sparking a lifelong interest that led him to work as a choir conductor and opera coach specializing in Russian music.

Michael Blackburn Forte remembers Mr. Lloyd forcibly impressing on him the need to learn more vocabulary and that when he left BGS he said he was the formative influence in developing his love of languages and that he has very fond memories of his teacher.

James Crookes sat next to his teacher at lunch in the school dining room and remembers being fascinated by his tales of travelling, his Cambridge years and his role in WWII.

Simon Hewitt remembers passing my father in the corridor before he became his teacher: 'With his deep-set eyes and Bobby Charlton-coiffed strands of grey hair, he looked frowningly austere'. However, later in the classroom, Simon's opinion of him changed. 'His eyes were a pale, piercing blue, and he liked to laugh…He had panache, charisma and a brain as big as a bullock: a palpably good man, with the naivety and wisdom of a holy fool'. It was Simon who copiously wrote what have become known as the *Clarence Quotes* and which you can read in Appendix VI.

I think I finally understood what a passionate and inspirational teacher my father was when Simon Hewitt sent me a link to a YouTube video of the Italian orchestra conductor, Claudio Abbado, conducting Gustav Mahler's Symphony No 1. He said: 'Go towards the end, 55:00, then watch the last two minutes. As Abbado conducted, so your father taught'. Watch it and you will understand. I did.

RETIREMENT

When I visited Bradford Grammar School in June 2019 to thank them for their contribution to the celebration of my father's 100th birth- day, Rebecca Bull, the Alumni Manager had dug out for me the 1983 Bradfordian magazine which includes a tribute to my father upon his retirement in the summer of 1983.

Written by his former head of department and close colleague, Harry Davis, I was touched to read the tribute which no doubt my father saw but never showed me. I would like to include it in this book edition as it gives yet another view of my father from his time at B.G.S. but this time from a teacher. Some of the facts of my father's early life are not quite correct but the important part is the description of his teaching at the school. So read on:

'Mr. C.C. Lloyd M.A.

Courtenay Lloyd was educated at Clifton and at Selwyn College, Cambridge, after which he spent three years working for the Imperi- al Tobacco Company (sic). During the war he served as Lieutenant in the R.N.V.R. and later in Naval Intelligence. Then, after a year with the British Naval Mission in Norway, for which he was awarded the Norwe- gian Freedom Medal, he spent two years in Schleswig-Holstein working with the Control Commission in Germany before doing his first spell of teaching: six years on the Joint Services Russian course in Cambridge, an intensive and highly successful course which produced a large number of teachers responsible for the launching of Russian as a school subject in this country. From Cambridge he went to teach Russian at the R.A.F.

College, Cranwell, where he spent a further six (sic) years before coming to B.G.S. as Senior Russian Master in January 1964.

We are very lucky indeed that such an outstanding scholar and linguist has stayed with us so long. His pupils have won top scholarships at Oxford and Cambridge, and we owe to him our reputation for excellence in Russian. At the same time his teaching of both French and German has been one of the most consistently successful features of the Modern Languages department.

His linguistic interests range widely, and boys in his Option courses on Scandinavian languages and, more recently, European languages in general, speak with admiration of the scope of his knowledge. Spain is his second home during the holidays and, not content with teaching in School, he takes part in Easter courses at Leeds University and summer courses at the University of East Anglia; he has also examined for the Institute of Linguists.

Roderick Thomson and I remember with great enjoyment the trips which we accompanied him to the Soviet Union. We had a generous staff ratio – 3 masters and 6 boys, though this did not protect us from the wrath of our Intourist guide when we overslept on the Red Arrow express from Leningrad to Moscow, and later failed to put our luggage on the correct floor for collection at the hotel: 'You are supposed to be intelligent people,' she shouted, her beautiful fur hat bobbling, 'why do you not do as you were told?' We also discovered that a tourist who speaks Russian without a trace of accent can sometimes be a liability; in the dining car everyone who ordered coffee in English was served immediately, whilst we, mistaken for Russians, had to wait in patience. In Moscow we were invited to the flat of the British Cultural Attaché (one of Courtenay's pupils of course), and a friend arrived with a large plastic carrier bag full of caviar and bottles of full strength (illegal) vodka brought from some unpronounceable place. We had a splendid evening, and David Whitlam led the singing with great feeling

....

After walking across Moscow through the frosty night air, spurned by taxi drivers, wewere accosted by several members of the oldest profession with enigmatic words: 'Goodbye, my love, goodbye'. Our only moment of real alarm dissolved in laughter: in the square outside the Hermitage in Leningrad, a grim-looking army officer, greatcoated and covered with badges of rank, fired a question at Courtenay, who, visibly relieved, was able to tell him that the go-kart racing started later in the afternoon.

The more official parts of our visits were fascinating, and Courtenay managed to get us tickets for several performances at the Bolshoi theatre, an achievement which we only truly appreciated when we steered our way through the groups of Russians trying to buy them from us in the street.

Courtenay Lloyd is a genuinely modest man, and I hope he will forgive me blowing his trumpet for him: it would never occur to him to do so himself. He is a totally committed teacher, and has always had the welfare of his pupils very much at heart, a fact which they all acknowledge with affection and respect. We will also miss him, and we wish him and Mrs. Elena Lloyd every happiness for the future. I am sure that the word 'retirement' for him will really mean an opportunity to get even more pleasure from his enthusiasm for languages. H. Davis'.

HIS DAUGHTER'S WEDDING IN MADRID.
21 August 1983

Freshly retired in the summer of 1983, Courtenay was happy to be able to concentrate on his daughter's wedding. Walking Masha down the aisle at her wedding was one of the proudest and happiest moments of his life.

Courtenay approved wholeheartedly of Eladio, his daughter's choice of husband. A Spanish teacher of philosophy and ex-Catholic priest sounded fine to him. He was to be another priest and another teacher in the family. Have you noticed how many priests, nuns and teachers there are in this biography? We were all surrounded by religion but none of us were real churchgoers. Later Eladio would be like a son to him. His full name, by the way, is Eladio Freijo Calzada.

COURTENAY LLOYD WALKING HIS DAUGHTER DOWN THE AISLE AT HER WEDDING. MADRID 21 AUGUST 1983.

When I met Eladio he didn't speak English. Soon after we met and fell in love in Callosa in 1980, I took him to Bradford to meet my parents. It was to be his first trip to England. On the train from Kings Cross to Bradford I taught him to say, 'How are you?' when he was to greet my father for the first time. When Courtenay Lloyd opened the door to the porch of 6 Heaton Grove, Eladio said: 'Who are you!' Being the gentleman he was, Mr. Lloyd replied politely, 'Very well, thank you'. It has remained a family joke forever after. Needless to say, later Eladio learned to speak English very well. He didn't have much choice in this family of linguists!

Below is a photograph of the family together, the last one taken with us all together. My father had the wedding cake made in England and brought it out to Spain personally. He also brought with him the English vicar who would officiate, the Very Reverend Brandon Jackson who was then the provost of Bradford Cathedral and later Dean of Lincoln and a close friend of the family. My parents were forever grateful to him for helping us when George got into trouble with the authorities as I will explain later.

THE FAMILY TOGETHER AT MASHA'S WEDDING. FROM LEFT TO RIGHT, ELENA, ELADIO, MASHA, COURTENAY AND GEORGE. MADRID 21 AUGUST 1983.

V

RETIREMENT IN ENGLAND AND IN SPAIN. 1983 TILL THE PRESENT DAY

RETIREMENT IN ENGLAND AND IN SPAIN.
1983 till the present day

Courtenay retired early in 1983. Elena retired a year or so later. They enjoyed travelling together and one of their first trips was to Berlin just after the wall fell. My father also took my mother to show her his beloved Finland which she enjoyed very much. However she never shared his love of what she called 'cold countries' and always yearned to visit Italy. Her revenge may have been when she bought the house in Callosa.

TO BULGARIA FOR A REUNION OF COURTENAY'S FOUR SISTERS-IN-LAW
46 years after the war (1990)

As the iron curtain began to disappear, in 1990 Elena decided it was time to return to Bulgaria where she had grown up after her family fled the Russian Revolution. Her older sister, Olga, a mother superior of a Russian Orthodox convent, still lived there. They were to meet for the first time since 1944. They were joined by their two other sisters, Daria a nun in New York and Masha the youngest. Courtenay and Aunty Masha joined Elena. As Aunty Masha was terrified of flying they went by train, crossing the whole of Europe. Apart from seeing her sisters, as well as old friends, her parents' house and her father's church, the main mission of that trip and a second one a year or so later was to give out relief gathered for the former communist country which was suffering huge deprivation. The Bradford newspaper, *The Telegraph and Argus*, wrote about the story which you can read in the clipping below.

To quote Elena in the article, she said about the reunion: 'We parted as young girls and only met again as old women'.

My father wrote an extensive diary of both trips. In the first one when my mother met her long lost sisters, I was dying to read his entry about their reunion but was disappointed as there was no emotion in the description. You see, he never was emotional but it must have been exciting to witness the reunion. I have kept these diaries and treasure them. Some bits of them are really rather funny. My father describes how they took lots of food out to give to the family they were staying with who were old friends of my aunt. One of the items was a Christmas pudding of all things and my father remembers how the family ate it without cooking it. He also remembers how people had to light fires to cook in the street as there were so many blackouts because the electricity was always down.

Apart from these trips, they mostly enjoyed their visits to Spain to stay with us and were overjoyed when they became grandparents. They didn't completely retire from teaching. Both of them continued to attend the Norwich Russian courses for quite a few years more, now under the leadership of Roy Bivon at the University of Essex, until they stopped.

A CLIPPING FROM *THE TELEGRAPH AND ARGUS* (BRADFORD PAPER) ABOUT THE REUNITING OF THE FOUR SISTERS IN BULGARIA IN 1990 AND THEIR APPEAL FOR THE 'FORGOTTEN PEOPLE'. FROM LEFT TO RIGHT: AUNTY MASHA, OLGA, ELENA AND DARIA. PUBLISHED 1 FEB 1991.

COURTENAY LLOYD'S WIFE, ELENA DIES
Bradford 1 October 1999

During their retirement Courtenay and Elena spent a quiet life in their rambling house in Bradford, reading the papers and their books, doing *The Times* crosswords and seeing friends. My father continued to do the shopping and preparing of meals as he had always done and I suspect that now it was just the two of them he rather liked the task. With Mr. Pearson's and Mr. Chaney's long gone, he now traipsed to Asda and back which was quite a distance. From Asda in Shipley he would go into the local library and bring books for my mother. He looked after her well as he had always done.

Their niece, Zuka, Elena's brother Kolya's daughter, and her husband Bruce, a Yorkshireman, would visit them often and take them delicious food. Then in the late 1990s Elena fell ill with cancer, a disease she dreaded. When she was in her fifties she had bowel cancer which was a huge scare. She was told she had three months to live but the doctors were wrong. This time, unfortunately, they were right and the diagnosis was breast cancer. Courtenay and Elena were very different in character but they doted on each other. He was to look after her until the end.

My father and I were both by her bed at the hospital when she was given her first dose of morphine in liquid form. She took the plastic glass, raised it to her mouth and said, 'Cheers' to the nurse. A chill went down my spine as I was forced to put on a smile. My mother's sense of humour never left her, not even when she was dying. Her last words to him in her native Russian were: 'Всё в порядке' (fsyo f poryádke), meaning 'everything is ok'. She went in peace and he was there with her as he had always been until she took her last breath, aged 79, at the Bradford

Royal Infirmary on 1 October 1999 when he became a widow. Being a good beast and suffering in silence, he went on stoically with his life and even travelled to his adored Nordic countries on solo trips. He carried on living in that massive house which was becoming far too big for him.

My mother is buried at Charlestown Cemetery in Baildon. My father and I are very grateful to my old school friend, Geraldine Howley, née Appleby, for putting flowers on Elena's grave when she visits her own parents' graves at the cemetery.

ELENA'S GRAVE AT CHARLESTOWN CEMETERY BAILDON.

COURTENAY LLOYD'S SON GEORGE DIES
London 15 May 2001

George with a huge talent for languages, music and sport was a 6ft tall, blonde and blue-eyed, extremely handsome boy. He was possibly an even better linguist than his parents and picked up languages in a matter of weeks, sounding in no time like a native of the country in question. He only had to hold a musical instrument and was immediately able to play it. He was even more charismatic than his mother and was generally loved by everyone, especially women because of his looks.

His first girlfriend and I suspect the love of his life, was a beautiful young Russian but British born girl called Tanya Bolashov, the daughter of Mr. Bolashov, lecturer at Bradford University. His family and ours were friends. George talked about her for years after they broke up even though he had many other girlfriends afterwards. I wonder where she is today. However, George was also

GEORGE - PHOTO TAKEN IN THE MID 1970s AT THE NORWICH RUSSIAN COURSES.

a troubled boy and in those days behavioural problems were generally misunderstood by the medical profession and left untreated.

Thus frustratingly none of his talents could be put to any use as he found it difficult to hold down a job. He inherited his parents' love of travel and had what he described as 'itchy feet'. Once he told our parents he was going to Paris for the weekend. In reality he had set off on foot and hitch-hiked all the way to Afghanistan. They didn't hear from him for a long time until a telegram came from the British Embassy in Kabul to say that George was in hospital with cholera. Courtenay and Elena sent the money for him to be repatriated and he arrived home with long hair, hardly any fat on his body and a great big sheepish grin on his face.

They loved him dearly but he would worry them many times, getting into trouble as a teenager and being expelled from any school he went to, including his father's school, Bradford Grammar, which must have been a huge embarrassment at the time. It must have been very sad for our father to have a troublesome boy as a son who dabbled in drugs while he taught brilliant and interested pupils at school. I think it often took the punch out of him and I wondered how he could go on. He always did though with his positive outlook on life.

After being expelled from BGS, my father found a place for him at the city's next best school, Fulneck. The problem with joining Fulneck was that it was very far from Heaton Grove and my father could no longer control his son. I remember their rows in the morning as George had to get up early and he hated getting out of bed. It must have been very stressful for my father. George would later 'skive' regularly, very often with Robin, the son of the owner of The Paddock, the fish and chip shop across the road from our house.

George's itchy feet later took him to Latin America which he explored from north to south and back again. Even in the 1970s it was dangerous and my parents were forever worried. He often got robbed and ran out of money and would ring my father on 'reversed charges,' giving him the number of a bank account to send money to which was invariably the wrong number. These calls would come during the middle of the night and the next day I would be marched with my parents to my mother's bank - for some funny reason they had separate bank accounts - to Barclays Bank on Market Street. I was needed to help with the Spanish while sending money to a bank in Bogota, Caracas or wherever. He came home eventually wearing a Peruvian poncho, once again with a great big sheepish grin on his handsome face.

Once in Callosa when my friend Amanda was staying with us she remembers seeing him in the street returning from one of his trips to South America. He looked shabby and dirty and in desperate need of a shower. His hair was a mess and his teeth had gone completely black. I told him off and amazingly the next day his teeth were suddenly gleaming white. I asked him how on earth that had happened. It seems he took the very drastic measure of using Vim to remove the black. Only George would have resorted to Vim to clean his teeth.

The biggest scare he ever gave my father and mother was when he left home without telling them, aged just seventeen. They didn't hear from him for at least three months and were worried sick. Even so, my poor dear father had to go and give his Russian lessons and perform in class while worried to death inside. I shall never forget his gaunt face during that dreadful period. Eventually they heard from him when he sent a letter from a prison in London asking them to bail him out. Imagine! He had joined a group of squatters who took him along when they robbed a shop. He had no idea where he was going but got caught all the same. Thanks to his being a first offender, and to the help of the Revd Brandon Jackson and our neighbour, the judge, Douglas Forrester-Paton who wrote good conduct letters to the judge, George was not sentenced. It was my sixteenth birthday on the day of his trial at the Bradford Magistrates' Court, not a good day to have a birthday. I went with my parents by bus to the courts and I shall never forget my father giving me £16 as a present, one for every year of my life. I felt so sorry for him at that moment.

My parents concentrated on George's difficult education and I was left to my own devices. I was not a good student, far preferring my social life. However even though I only generally scraped through at school or had scathing reports with some pretty negative comments from teachers such as 'Maria (as I was called at school and hated) is a *minimum* girl,' I did not worry my parents too much as George's issues were far more acute. I was even mentioned in Amanda's glowing reports - she would go on to study at Oxford - and shall never forget when they wrote, 'Good away from Maria'. It made me cringe at the time and still does today. What also made me cringe was being referred to as Maria. As I have explained elsewhere in this book, most Marias or Marys in Russia are called by the diminutive and more informal name "Masha" and that's how I like to be called. In fact, if someone calls out the name Maria, as happens at doctors' surgeries for example, I simply don't register as Maria for me is only my name on paper. My mother always told me she named me after St. Mary of Egypt, known in her early life as a great sinner. I have always wondered why. I did not have the privilege of teachers like my father and should have benefited more from his knowledge.

I do remember though, just when O levels were coming up, he had to prep me for French. I spoke it quite well but my grammar and spelling were appalling. In about three weeks he got me up to standard and I passed. I think I learned more French in those three weeks than I did in three years at St. Joseph's College. Eventually I pulled my finger out and only in my last year at Nottingham University where I studied Spanish or rather Hispanic Studies, did I really swat and amazingly managed to graduate with a 2:1 and a distinction in spoken Portuguese. It was rather a feather in my cap to have learned just one language neither my parents nor my brother knew. I think my father was proud of that too.

George passed his A levels in French and German with straight As but didn't have to swat at all. As I said earlier, he was very good at picking up languages. I also said at the beginning of this biography that my father is shy and bad at expressing his feelings. Thus he could never discuss intimate things such as sex with us. Once, my brother asked my father to tell him 'the facts of life'. My father famously replied, 'Get on with your German verbs!'

We never saw our father in any intimate situation and God forbid, ever naked. He would never hug or kiss us, he was too shy for that and would feel embarrassed but that didn't mean he didn't love us. On the contrary, he adored us but just couldn't tell us so. My mother was quite the opposite and we would spend many an hour at her side in the bathroom at 6 Heaton Grove while she enjoyed bathing in the huge Victorian claw-footed bath tub with a cigarette forever in her hand. Amanda, my friend, vividly remembers my mother taking her one day conspiratorially into the bathroom where she showed her a massive mountain of cigarette ends that had accumulated, hidden behind the far side of the bath tub. It made her laugh and laugh and it made me laugh too remembering that mountain. I now remember that when I was older and also smoked, I did the same. It was my poor father who would remove them all when he did the house cleaning.

George managed to get a degree in Latin American Studies at Portsmouth Polytechnic before he was hit with a diagnosis of full blown schizophrenia. Suddenly his previous behaviour made sense and now he could get some treatment for his condition.

In his thirties he went to London and ended up living in a home run by an NGO called Umbrella in Belsize Park for people with a similar condition. There he met his future wife, a young and disturbed but extremely intelligent Serbian girl called Sanya. She had graduated with a degree in philosophy from Belgrade University but was never able to be happy or fit into society as she had been brutally abused as a child. But she found happiness, albeit short-lived, when she met my brother. Amazingly they fell in love and it really was true love. They married quietly in February 1999 in Camden (London) and only told our parents after the event. Their marriage, sadly, would be very brief. When the medical staff informed my father, Sanya and I that George had melanoma and just a few months to live it was a huge blow for all of us but especially for Sanya. I would fly out from Madrid every Saturday

GEORGE AND SANYA ON THEIR WEDDING DAY, 1998.

in the months leading up to his death and meet my father at King's Cross. With heavy hearts we would take the tube to Belsize Park where we would visit George, together with Sanya, first at the London Free Hospital and later at a hospice called Eden House in Hampstead. After George's death, Courtenay would travel up to London once a month and he and Sanya would visit George's grave together. They became quite close. Sanya never knew it but her father-in-law had made a provision for her in his will. Our only consolation was that George had not died when my mother was still alive. She would not have been able to bear it. My father being the good beast who suffers in silence, had no choice but to carry on. Now only he and I were left of the family my parents had formed during those happy days in Cambridge.

When Sanya heard those dreaded words from the doctor, she cried out, 'I can't live without him!' That was totally true. She could not live without him. She cared for him until his death on 15 May 2001, never leaving his side. She looked a stark, young widow dressed in black at the gloomy Serbian Orthodox funeral.

As for me, I had lost my only brother. I will forever feel guilty at being the sibling who received all the luck and that he had none. Despite all his talents - he was better at everything than I was - he was dealt very bad cards and I was dealt the best. I also feel guilty for not having cared for him more in my life. When he was a troubled boy at home and afterwards I could not acknowledge he was mentally ill. I was cross with him for being a burden on my parents. Only at the end of his life did I really understand and I am forever glad we made our peace and that I finally understood that his behavioural problems were not his fault. I think my father thinks similarly. Oh, if I only I had done more for him. Please forgive me George, my darling golden brother.

GEORGE'S WIFE, SANYA LLOYD, NÉE JANCIC, DIES.
London 17 October 2008

After he died I tried to keep in touch with Sanya. Whenever I went to London on a business trip I went to see her, taking her chocolates, perfume and cigarettes out of guilt, I suppose. On one of my first visits, I sat and hugged her as she cried and told me how much she missed my brother. She also told me her life story full of abuse which I do not want to reproduce here as it is too sad. She cried too for the children she had never had and I can't tell you how much I felt for her. As I hugged her hard I realized that no one had ever really loved her until she met my brother and that in order to blossom all she really needed was love. I kept in contact, sending her presents at Christmas and even invited her to stay with us in Madrid. But she wouldn't dare fly. There was not much I could do to help and I have always regretted not doing more.

About seven years later I got a phone call from the police in London which came as a terrible shock. They asked me if I knew Sanya Lloyd which I confirmed, then they asked if I was alone and would I please sit down. I still wasn't prepared when the police officer on the other end of the line told me she had been found dead in her flat on 17 October 2008. I asked if she had committed suicide. She said the cause of death was pneumonia. Later when I talked to the Anglican vicar at the church she attended, he told me it was he who had found her when she didn't turn up for church twice in a row. In his mind and in my mind, she got pneumonia but had lost the will to live and let herself die. Oh, how dreadful to die like that on her own. When I put the receiver down I had to go and tell my father of yet one more death in the family, another blow.

He took it as he always does, stoically, but nodding sadly. He would suffer in silence once again.

My father was too old by then to go to her funeral so I went on behalf of us both. It was very sombre and sad. Poignantly they both died at the age of 46. They are buried together at the St. Pancras and Islington Cemetery in East Finchley. Their joint grave can be found at these coordinates: 1 x Number 192.

My other consolation was that they both found love at the end of their lives, even though it was short-lived.

GEORGE AND SANYA ARE BURIED TOGETHER IN EAST FINCHLEY.

LAST TRIP TO RUSSIA - THE LIEVEN READINGS
Voskresensk (Near Moscow) 2003

Soon after my mother died, my father made his last trip to Russia. It was to attend the *Lieven Readings*. Amazingly, long after communism had fallen, a group of people wanted to pay homage to my mother's family. My father was accompanied by his two sisters-in-law, Aunty Masha and Aunty Valya, (the wife of my mother's brother, Kolya) although they travelled separately to Moscow. The trip was a huge occasion for them as they were to see for the first time the estate the Lieven family lived on.

He flew to Moscow as Voskresensk is only 80 kilometres away and stayed at the Rossiya hotel which he said is perhaps the largest hotel in the world. He describes it as a 'typical soulless Soviet-style construction built in the 1960s'. The night before going to Voskresensk, he visited the centre of Moscow and was furious to see the Red Square was closed due to a concert to be given by that 'foul-mouthed sentimental 61-year old ex-Beatle, Sir *(he crosses out the 'Sir')* Paul McCartney, a drug-taker as well'. My father hated the Beatles and all they represented. I did laugh at his description of the group's vocalist.

They were wined and dined as aristocracy and my Aunty Masha came into her own. The three of them enjoyed every minute of the occasion and never forgot the trip. Today these mansions are in the hands of the state. Many people have asked us if we could ever claim them back. Well, no, not in Putin's Russia and how could we prove ownership? In order to document this trip I have had the very reliable source of my father's diary of his visit. He says in it 'what a great experience for me so late in life. If only poor Mummy could have been present'.

MY FATHER WITH AUNTY MASHA AND AUNTY VALYA
AT THE LIEVEN READINGS IN 2003.

SPASSKOYE HOUSE THE LIEVEN FAMILY HOME ON THE KRIVYAKINO ESTATE IN
VOSKRESENSK NEAR MOSCOW WHICH BELONGED
TO MY MATERNAL GRANDFATHER.

The *Lieven Readings* were inspired by Misha Kozmenko. He had been the editor and publisher of my grandfather's poetry and writings which my mother typed up from his manuscripts. One is called *Lyrika* and contains his poems, and the other is *The Lives of the Saints*. It was my mother's lifelong ambition to publish them. It was Misha who was inspired to organize the *Lieven Readings* to honour the family's efforts in improving medical and educational services in the region.

It must have been easy for the Lieven family with all their riches and contacts to help the locals in the town of Voskresensk which, by the way, was only one of their princely estates in Russia. According to my father's diary, they visited the Lieven properties on the estate of Krivyakimo, first to the house belonging to my grandfather's sister and then to my grandfather's own home, The Spasskoye House, much larger than the former. They are very imposing buildings.

Both properties were turned into children's homes during the communist regime and are completely run down now.

In his diary, my father cites Aunty Masha. It was for her, after so many impressions, 'two days of elation and sadness'. As for him, he says, 'What a totally surprising and unexpected visit to Russia it has been, absolutely memorable, such an extraordinary warm welcome'.

HE MOVES TO SPAIN TO LIVE IN MADRID
WITH HIS DAUGHTER MASHA AND FAMILY
October 2005

After the death of his wife and son, Courtenay soldiered on until the house just got too big for him. In 2004 we persuaded him to leave 6 Heaton Grove where he had lived for forty years. He sold the house a year later and went to live in Madrid with his daughter, the only family he had left.

My father had lived at the old house in Bradford for so long and moving was a slow process. There was so much stuff to get rid of, sell, give away or send to Spain. Eladio and I were there for the last week helping him, and I remember very clearly the last two nights at 6 Heaton Grove as I imagine he does too. He had sold the house to Mr Nawaz who already owned several houses on the street and who had been angling to buy my father's even when my mother was alive. The selling process, although long, had gone quite smoothly and we were very touched when my father's purchaser invited us to dinner at his house on the last night but one. I think it was to be the first time and maybe the last that my father had ever eaten curry. My mother and George loved curry as do Eladio and I but my father has never been keen on it. We arrived at their house which was the one opposite ours and richly decorated in deep reds and golds and were courteously shown all around it. There seemed to be many people living there. Then we were ushered into the dining room to see a table laden with beautiful Pakistani delicacies, none of which I knew my father would like.

I was a bit thrown when our host told us he was leaving us as he had to go to the mosque and that he couldn't eat as it was Ramadan. It was the strangest thing to be invited to dinner and then left to eat it all alone. When we protested - my father never said a word - he brought in his eldest daughter and said she would be our hostess, but she did not eat either. We enjoyed authentic homemade curry though the desserts were all from Asda - those my father did enjoy. Our hostess was a delightful girl who had just got a degree from Bradford University but I can't remember in what subject. She told us while we ate that she had just married her cousin and was getting to know him over the phone. I politely asked if she wouldn't prefer to live with him in his country. She said 'oh no' as they enjoyed a much higher standard of living in England. I could sympathize especially after seeing the two stretch limousines in their driveway. It was the most bizarre dinner and when we finished I think if I had offered my father a stiff drink he would have swallowed it one go.

On his last night in Bradford, and for the first time in our lives, we were invited to dinner by our closest neighbours, the Wrights, who had lived next door to us ever since we moved into 6 Heaton Grove. Marguerite Wright who was about to turn a hundred and died at 104, lived with her younger daughter, Susan Wright, a spinster aged about 80. Naturally the food that night was very different and catered perfectly to my father's taste. The Wrights had always been very good neighbours and dinner at their house proved to be the perfect send off for my father who would leave for Spain the next day.

So in October 2005, and he remembers the exact date, escorted by Eladio and myself, he flew from Manchester to Madrid to live with us and his granddaughters and to begin a whole new life, this time in Spain.

As you will read in the last part of the book, *About the Author*, I am a PR professional in the telecoms sector in Spain. My husband, Eladio Freijo is an ex-Catholic priest who was born in Montrondo, a small village in the north of Spain, and is the eldest of six siblings. With just 12 or so permanent dwellers, it is located in a very mountainous and rural region in the province of León in north-west Spain. His village where we have restored the old family house is very important to all of us and my father loves it. He has spent many a pleasant time there with us, climbing the mountains and admiring the forest of birch trees, his favourite tree from his time in Scandinavia when he was a young man. Eladio later went on to become a teacher of philosophy although he is now retired.

He and my father always got on and my husband has become like a son to my father, caring for him so well in his old age. My father is very proud of his two granddaughters, Suzy and Olivia. Suzy is a nutritionist and dietitian and worked until recently for the NHS in London. But after six years there she upped and left for Bali in the summer of 2018 to 'lead a simpler life'. Following in her grandparents' footsteps, she recently became a successful online teacher of English to Chinese children.

Olivia, our youngest daughter lives in Madrid and is a reporter for TVE, Spain's national broadcaster. At the time of writing Olivia was expecting a baby boy to be called Elliot. My father approved saying Elliot was a very distinguished name and soon a new member of the family would be born. thus my father became a great grandfather in September 2019 and I was so happy for him. Both girls cherish their grandfather and have given him much joy. He follows their lives with great interest. When we talk to Suzy on Skype, he does too and is always amazed at the new technology available today. He is forever interested in any new advances in this field, for example, asking me to explain what Facebook and Twitter are. I try

IN A WINERY IN LA RIOJA WITH HIS FAMILY IN SPAIN. FROM LEFT TO RIGHT, OLIVIA, MASHA, COURTENAY, ELADIO AND SUZY. NOVEMBER 2009.

hard to answer him. It's such a pity he was a little too old to embrace the World Wide Web when it was invented as it would have fascinated him and kept him in touch real time with what is going on in the world. However, he keeps well abreast with world news via traditional media, the TV and his books.

My father adapted well to Spain, knowing the language and loving the country and being very interested in its history. As a teenager he had followed the events of the Spanish Civil War with fascination.

After moving here and now aged 87, he went on solo trips to Norway, Denmark and Finland. We also took him on holiday with us everywhere, both in Spain and back to England, and he enjoyed a trip to Cornwall and revisiting Yorkshire. He got to know Spain quite well on holidays with Eladio and me to Cáceres, Badajoz, Trujillo, Córdoba, Granada, Mérida and Gredos and many other places. And of course he came with us many times to Eladio's village, Montrondo and to our apartment near Alicante, an area he knows well from our 'Callosa days'.

PHOTO TAKEN AT OUR OLD HOUSE IN MADRID
JUST AFTER MY FATHER CAME TO LIVE WITH US.

We even took him to Gibraltar which he had last seen during the war. There, we stayed at the Rock Hotel, an iconic building on the island, in its day a magnet for royalty and the rich and famous. Today it has lost a lot of its glamour and is a little rundown. Some of its most famous guests have included Winston Churchill, Errol Flynn, Sir Alex Guinness, Sean Connery, John Lennon and Yoko Ono. How interesting for my father to stay at the hotel where Sir Winston Churchill, Great Britain's WWII prime minister had once stayed. However, as my father was never a fan of the Beatles, those particular past guests did not impress him so much. He enjoyed his return to Gibraltar immensely and it must have brought back memories of the war when his ship would anchor there. We got very worried though when one of the tiresome monkeys landed on his shoulder although it didn't ruffle him a bit.

We also took him to Galicia, that lovely region in north-west Spain with a rugged coastline that would remind him of Scotland or Yorkshire. If in England, Yorkshire is often called 'God's own country', Galicia in Spain is considered similarly by its native 'Gallegos'. Below is a photo of him at the wonderful *parador* in Baiona in the province of Pontevedra in an area called Las Rías Bajas (the low fjords) where we stayed in the summer of 2008. He was in his element here, enjoying the walks, and I love him in his panama hat, ever the English gentleman discovering new places to travel to.

In Spain we would stay at some of the majestic state-run *parador* hotels, like the one in Baiona, which are often converted historic buildings such as monasteries or castles. Here he loved to stay in at night and order room service. My father always appreciated the good life. I remember as a child him talking about how lovely meals were if served on a white tablecloth which of course never happened at home as meals were served on the pink formica table in the kitchen. At the *paradors* he got his wish.

Unfortunately in his mid-nineties he broke his hip. He had a replacement but never walked again. He never complained but it must have pained him as he had always loved walking. It meant also he needed the help of others which he had to resign himself to but which I'm sure he never accepted. Who would?

WITH MY FATHER IN BOBADILLA IN THE PROVINCE OF GRANADA, MARCH 2008.

COURTENAY WITH HIS PANAMA HAT AT THE PARADOR IN BAIONA,
PONTEVEDRA SUMMER OF 2008.

During his time with us, he didn't completely give up teaching. When Olga, a young Paraguayan woman was hired to be his carer he gave her English lessons and she became quite proficient. He also gave Russian lessons to my great friend Fátima Sánchez's brother Manolo. Both Olga and Manolo recognized in my father the teacher he had been. He may have been old but he hadn't lost his touch.

While talking to him about his past and his ancestors for this book, he told me, 'When I am in bed, I am always thinking about the past'. I replied that I was too while writing about him and how I hadn't listened to him when I was younger. His reply was so generous. He said, 'Well, why would you?' He understood me completely. I am only glad it wasn't too late that I finally listened to the man who gave me my life.

VI

TURNING
ONE HUNDRED -
RECOGNITION FOR
A WWII VETERAN
1 MAY 2019

TURNING ONE HUNDRED –
RECOGNITION FOR A WWII VETERAN
1 May 2019

When he approached his hundredth birthday, he had many amazing memories. to look back on.

He may think his life was very ordinary but after writing this biography I can only say that it was actually quite extraordinary.

For an Englishman to be such a polyglot is a feat in itself. However, as there are so few of them left, I think it is as a veteran of WWII that we should afford him the greatest recognition and all wish him hearty congratulations.

2019 was the 80th anniversary of the start of WWII and we should never forget.

Courtenay Lloyd fought for his country and for peace and the unity of Europe and deserves to be remembered.

Congratulations on your centenary Daddy, Grandpa, Mr. Lloyd, Mr. C.C. Lloyd, Mr. Lloyd, Courtenay, Court, Clarence, Courtenay Lloyd, you will always be well remembered and we are happy to have you with us.

You are the best father a daughter could wish for.

APPENDIX I

COURTENAY LLOYD'S FAMILY TREE

Evan William Lloyd (1828 -)

Martha Fox (1834 -)

Grace Parry (1829 - 1901)

Sarah Harrington (1819 - 1895)

John Collins (1829 - 1904)

Ellen (1828

Annie Fox Lloyd (1868 - 1942)

Thomas Fox Lloyd (1871 - 1927)

William Fox Lloyd (1860 - 1936)

Marian M. Collins (1862 - 1940)

David John Collins (1854 - 1912)

Elian Emily Pemberton MBE (1858 - 1945)

Jame (1

William Fox Lloyd (1890 - 1973)

Gwendolyn Price Hughes (1890 - 1970)

Thomas Breese (1894 - 1970)

Ellen (Nellie) Lloyd (1893 - 1988)

Thomas Fox Lloyd (1897 - 1971)

Lillie (Peggy) Kn (1894 - 1984

Blodwen Price Fox Lloyd (1918 - 1964)

James Murray

Gwendolyn Elizabeth Fox Lloyd (1921 - 1990)

Norman Woolstenhulme (- 2008)

William Evan Fox Lloyd (1925 - 1993)

Katriona Ishbel Macleod ((1921 - 2001)

Arthur H. Radford (1900 - 1983)

Mona Lloyd (1927 - 2(

Pamela Lloyd Murray (1945 -)

Norman Lloyd Woolstenhulme (1964)

Katriona Fox Lloyd (1953 -)

Paul Mallon

Jennifer Lloyd Radford (1950 -)

George Lloyd (1955 - 2001)

Jack Fox Lloyd Mallon

n Frawley Pte

Henry Scull
(1822 - 1899)

Maria Stone
(1819 - 1879)

William Walters
(1841 -)

Keturah Annie
Gough (1849 - 1901)

George Frawley
(1847 - 1852)

Mary Ann Frawley
(1850 - 1861)

Charles E. Scull
(1862 - 1921)

Elizabeth G. Walters
(1868 - 1943)

Lloyd
16)

John Collins Lloyd
(1887 - 1961)

Dorothy Gertrude Scull
(1892 - 1970)

Walter Williams
(1892 - 1970)

Gwendoline B. Scull
(1898 - 1961)

Harold Benson
(1893 - 1927)

d

Elena (Helen) Von
Lieven (1920 - 1999)

Raymond W. Lloyd
(1922 - 1938)

Derek Orchard
(1930 - 1971)

Gloria E Lloyd
(1926 - 1971)

Angela Benson
(1924)

Freijo Calzada
(1944)

Maria (Masha)
Lloyd (1957)

Jacqueline M. Orchard
(1959 - 1971)

Michael J. Orchard
(1962 - 1971)

Antony W. Orchard
(1964 - 1971)

a Freijo Lloyd
(1984)

Olivia Freijo Lloyd
(1985)

Miguel Ángel
García Bermejo
(1975)

APPENDIX II

COURTENAY LLOYD'S IMMEDIATE FAMILY AND ANCESTORS

FATHER: JOHN COLLINS LLOYD

Revd Canon John Collins Lloyd. Born 13 November 1887, Holyhead, Anglesey, Wales.

Died 19 March 1961, Ickenham, Middlesex aged 74. Graduated St. David's College, Lampeter (Wales) c.1910. Entered the church, became a canon.

COURTENAY LLOYD'S FATHER, JOHN COLLINS LLOYD - CHAPLAIN TO THE FORCES IN WWI.

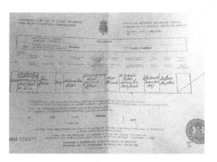

COURTENAY'S FATHER'S BIRTH CERTIFICATE.

PATERNAL GRANDFATHER
WILLIAM FOX LLOYD

William Fox Lloyd. Born Liverpool July 1860, of Welsh extraction on both sides. He served in the Merchant Navy in WWI and was awarded various medals for his services, including the British War medal. Katriona, his granddaughter has kept records of these medals. It is wonderful to see how members of my father's family contributed to the success of their country in the Great War just as Courtenay would in WWII.

Ironically, Courtenay would follow in the footsteps of his grandfather by joining the navy and would get a medal too but from a different king.

JOHN COLLINS LLOYD'S FATHER'S WWI MEDALS
AS A SEAMAN IN THE MERCHANT NAVY.

Courtenay's paternal grandfather was also a Freemason in the Llangefni Lodge (Anglesey). His lifelong job though was as a steward on the Holyhead ferry to Dublin where later he would become chief steward.

WILLIAM FOX LLOYD SENIOR (MY FATHER'S GRANDFATHER) AS CHIEF STEWARD ON THE HOLYHEAD TO DUBLIN FERRY. HE IS THE CAPTAIN IN THE MIDDLE OF THE PHOTO SURROUNDED BY HIS CREW.

Barry Hillier, a trustee of the Holyhead Maritime Museum informed me that William Fox Lloyd senior joined the LNWR (London and North Western Railway Company) in 1880. It seems the LNWR passenger steamers were taken over by the Admiralty in WWI for service and that William Fox Lloyd was on the *Anglia* and then volunteered for the *Cambria* which was converted to a hospital ship. He was not wounded in action in the war.

PATERNAL GRANDMOTHER MARIAN MARGARET COLLINS AND HER FATHER JOHN COLLINS

MY FATHER'S IRISH
GRANDMOTHER
(PATERNAL)
BORN IN INDIA,
MARIAN MARGARET
COLLINS.

Marian Margaret Collins was born in the British Raj, Delhi in 1862 and died in Anglesey in 1940. Marian Margaret Collins's parents were Irish; John Collins from Tralee and Ellen Frawley from Kerry. That means my father had a grandmother of Irish origin and Irish great grandparents and may still qualify for an Irish passport (*** see Marian Margaret Collins's brother David John Collins).

Her father, John Collins (born Tralee, Ireland 1827, died Holyhead 1904), was in the 82nd Regiment of Foot. With his regiment he travelled the world and his family followed him everywhere. He was an eyewitness to the Charge of the Light Brigade and returned to Great Britain to live in Anglesey He was awarded three medals: the Crimean Medal (with clasp, for the Siege of Sebastopol), the Turkish Medal, and the Indian Mutiny Medal (with clasp for the Defence of Lucknow). Courtenay remembers these tales of his exploits from his father when he was a boy. My cousin, Katriona Fox Lloyd, told me that our great, great grandfather, John Collins had been offered money to educate his offspring as part of his awards. He used the money to educate his son, David John Collins Margaret Marian Collins' brother, (read more about him below) who would become one of the most important surveyors in the British Empire. It seems my father's great grandfather was quite a character and a well-known figure in Holyhead. On his return from battle he bought a pub, The Sydney Inn where he became the landlord and would get into the odd scrape. But he was considered a local hero and when he died his funeral was well attended and he was given a hero's send-off. According to his obituary in a local paper, 'A firing party of volunteers preceded the cortege and fired three volleys over his grave'. The chief mourners were his family, including his grandchildren, John Collins Lloyd, William Fox Lloyd, Ellen Lloyd, Thomas Fox Lloyd and Owen Noel Lloyd, all mentioned in the cutting. But the whole town must have turned out. He is buried in the town cemetery in Maeshyfryd.

A VETERAN'S DEATH.—On Friday morning, after a short illness, the death took place at his daughter's residence, Mrs Lloyd, 26, Cambrian street, of John Collins, an old Crimean veteran, at the age of 76. The deceased, as a soldier in the 82nd Foot, took part in the Indian Mutiny and the Crimean war. He was an eye-witness of the charge of the Light Brigade. He held three medals,—Indian Mutiny and Crimean, and the Turkish medal. The funeral took place on Monday at the Maeshyfryd Cemetery, the Rev D. Basil Jones officiating. A firing party of the local Volunteers preceded the cortege and fired three volleys over the grave. The chief mourners were Mr and Mrs Lloyd (daughter and son-in-law), John Willie, Thomas, Noel and Nellie Lloyd (grand-children). Following the carriage were Mr John Murch, R.N., Mr Scudamore, Mr W. D. Jones, C.C., Mr Josiah T. Griffith, Mr R. O. Earl, Mr R. Williams, Thomas street; Mr John Williams, Careg Domos; Mr Steele, Mr Williams, Cambrian street; Mr Cotton, C.E.,; Mr O. H. Griffith, Alderley terrace; Mr Owen Griffith, Stanley street; Mr Henry Jones, Hill street; &c. Mrs Owen Hughes, Careg Domos, was the undertaker.

THE OBITUARY OF JOHN COLLINS, MY FATHER'S
GREAT GRANDFATHER, VETERAN OF CRIMEAN WAR
AND INDIAN MUTINY.

THE SHORT STORY OF COURTENAY'S FATHER, JOHN COLLINS LLOYD

19 ALDERLEY TERRACE, HOLYHEAD, THE FAMILY HOME OF JOHN COLLINS LLOYD.

My father remembers his own father's family address in Holyhead perfectly. It was 19 Alderley Terrace. At the time of writing this biography I saw that the five-bedroom terrace house was on sale for £125,000.

My friend, Joanne Wilcock recently visited the house and described it to me. It is a large five-bedroom, three-storey house with views to the ferry terminal (Holyhead to Dublin). His father, William Fox Lloyd, worked as chief steward on the ferries so he wouldn't have had far to go to work.

His father is also listed in the Wales Census of 1881 as being part of the crew on the SS *Shamrock* which was a paddle steamer which ran from 1876 to 1898.

The house has a view of the sea from the upper floors and is a short walk from the beach. There are a lot of the original fixtures such as the bannister and porch tiles. In short, a bargain for such a well-situated and large house. Maybe I should buy it.

However, John Collins Lloyd was not born at that house. Believe it or not, he was born in a pub, The Sydney Inn, now called The Dublin Packet. It is one in a row of five pubs called The Five Sisters on the Rhos y Gaer Terrace in Holyhead.

THE OLD SYDNEY INN WHERE JOHN COLLINS LLOYD WAS BORN.

THE PRIMARY SCHOOL JOHN COLLINS WENT TO IN HOLYHEAD,
THE OLD BRITISH SCHOOL.

So, my grandfather was born in a pub! The pub was bought by his grandfather, John Collins upon his return from the Indian Mutiny and other battles with his regiment. No doubt, apart from spending his award money on the education of his offspring, he also became a landlord of The Sydney Inn. His own son, William Fox Lloyd senior, must have inherited the pub. However, as we know he went on to become the chief steward of the ship that went from Holyhead to Dublin; the family would have sold the pub and then moved elsewhere in town.

As a young boy my grandfather went to The Old British School, a primary school near Alderley Terrace which no longer exists, where he earned a choral scholarship to New College Oxford. There he would sing in the university college choir and be educated at New College School.

He always had a good voice and was very musical. The Welsh are well known for their passion for rugby but also for their singing and sometimes Wales is referred to as the 'land of song'. It's part of their tradition and identity.

As a boy of somewhat humble origins, it must have been a great honour for him to win this scholarship and attending New College School, no doubt, gave him the best education possible. It is one of the oldest schools in England and was founded in 1379 to provide choristers for the chapel of New College Oxford. According to the college Register of Choristers, John Collins Lloyd was selected in July 1899 and joined the choir in October of that year when he was aged eleven. He was a boarder and pupil of New College School and the college paid half of his boarding costs at the beginning of his choristership, later paying the full fees until he left the choir in 1902. He was a boy treble and left when his voice broke at the age of fourteen. As a boarder this would have taken him away from his family but his time there would have been a great privilege for him. It would have been a very hard and disciplined life too as the role of a chorister at New College School was not an easy one. According to the book, *New College School, Oxford: A History*, by the current Deputy Head, Matthew Jenkinson, the headmaster of the time was was known as 'the formidable George Carter'. He ran the school with an iron rod but was a good teacher. There were some twenty-four choristers who lived with the headmaster and his family at 19 Holywell Street. The location was stunning; right next to the Bodleian Library. The boys dined with the family

6 NEW COLLEGE LANE. THE SCHOOLHOUSE BUILT c. 1870 AND THE LOCATION OF THE SCHOOL UNTIL 1903.

and shared the bathroom. Apparently the food was awful and the choristers must have gone hungry. I'm sure my grandfather pined for his mother's cooking. Sometimes, the Wednesday and Friday litany was so long the pupils fainted as a result of their empty stomachs. Their schooling took place nearby at 6 New College Lane and their days were very full. They were up at 7.15 a.m. and in Chapel by 8 a.m. Breakfast was apparently small and lessons began at 9 a.m. and finished at 11.50 a.m. The choristers then returned to the college for three-quarters of an hour for choir practice. Lunch followed and then there was sport until 3 p.m. After sport the choristers resumed their lessons until 4.30 p.m. in time for evensong at

5 p.m. Tea was at 6 p.m. followed by two hours of homework, piano practice and finally games. The choristers hardly had any free time in their long days; just games before going to bed. Bedtime was at 9 p.m.

JOHN COLLINS LLOYD (IN THE MIDDLE) WITH ONE OF HIS CHOIRS.

John Collins Lloyd's musical education would serve him well when he set up his own church choirs later in life at his different parish churches.

Upon his return from Oxford he became a pupil at the Holyhead Grammar School, just a short walk from his home in Alderley Terrace.

Perhaps those early years linked to the church stirred in him the beginnings of what would turn into a vocation and make him decide to become a clergyman. He studied theology at St. David's College, Lampeter, graduating in 1910. This Welsh university is now called the University of Wales after merging with Trinity University College. It was founded in 1828 specifically as a college where Welsh ordinands could receive a higher education which would have made it the obvious choice for my grandfather. Here is a photo of him on graduation day.

COURTENAY'S FATHER, JOHN COLLINS LLOYD, ON GRADUATION DAY AT ST. DAVID'S COLLEGE LAMPETER 1910.

According to an article in a local newspaper, the Carnarvon and Denbigh Herald and North and South Wales Independent, dated 1 July 1910, he graduated with a first-class degree. The same article also mentions the New College Oxford choral scholarship he won when he was a pupil at the Old British School.

SUCCESS.—Mr J. Collins Lloyd, son of Mr and Mrs Lloyd, Alderley Terrace, has obtained a first class in the final examination for the B.A. degree. Mr Lloyd is an old pupil of Mr W. J. Owen, having received his early education at the Old British School whence he obtained a scholarship at New College School, Oxford.

ARTICLE ON JOHN COLLINS LLOYD ACHIEVING A FIRST-CLASS
DEGREE AND A CHORAL SCHOLARSHIP
TO NEW COLLEGE OXFORD.

The family church was the thirteenth century parish church of St. Cybi in Holyhead, primarily a Welsh speaking church, and in some of the censuses of the time the family is listed as bilingual. However, I doubt they spoke it naturally at home because my great grandfather was born in Liverpool and my great grandmother, who was born in Delhi, was of Irish origin. My father further confirmed this, saying his father had learned it at Sunday school but that English was the language they spoke at home. We have a newspaper clipping from 1903 with the results of the Sunday School Examinations which further confirms that the family worshipped at St. Cybi's. John Collins Lloyd must have been a good student as he comes second in the list of pupils' results. His next brother down, William Fox Lloyd Junior, is also on the list.

CLASS D.—SUNDAY SCHOOL SCHOLARS UNDER 16
YEARS OF AGE.
FIRST CLASS.

1	Elizeus G. Parry, Criccieth ...	..	98	85	87	270
2	John Collins Lloyd, S. Cybi, Holyhead ..		88	76	80	244
3	Thomas Wooding, S. James, Bangor	..	67	83	93	243
4	Ethel Madge Murch, S. Seiriol, Holyhead		82	84	75	241
5	Menai Jones, S. James, Bangor	..	86	70	78	234
6	John C. Rowlands, Amlwch	..	77	71	84	232
7	Wm. Fox Lloyd, S. Cybi, Holyhead		87	82	62	231
8	Maggie Rowlands (W), Llanddyfnan	..	71	71	80	222
9	M. Gladys T. Williams, S. David, Bangor		81	59	76	216
10	William O. Parry, Criccieth ..		79	74	60	213
11	Alice B. Griffith, Llanddyfnan..	..	70	77	65	212
	Cordelia M. Jones, Glanogwen .	..	73	58	81	212
13	Mary Smith, S. Seiriol, Holyhead	..	60	76	75	211
	William Thomas, S. James, Bangor	..	71	61	79	211
15	Gomer V. Humphreys (W), Maentwrog..		75	71	64	210
	George H. Walker, S. James, Bangor	..	65	66	79	210

JOHN COLLINS LLOYD DID WELL AT WELSH AS CAN BE SEEN
IN THESE EXAMINATION RESULTS FROM
ST. CYBI'S CHURCH FOR 1903.

My father still has his Welsh bible along with some of the works of *The Mabinogion* (the earliest stories of British literature, compiled in Middle Welsh in the twelfth and thirteenth centuries). The latter must have come from his time at university rather than from Sunday school.

Shortly afterwards, he entered holy orders and was ordained first as deacon on 18 December 1910, and one year later as priest on 21 December 1911 in the Anglican Church, the Church of England. His ordination as a priest was officiated by the Bishop of Bangor, Alfred George, and took place at St Asaph Cathedral.

After he was ordained, he joined his first parish as curate at St. Mary's Church in the famous Welsh town of Lannfairpwll. It's famous because of its long name, the second longest name for a town in the world.

The full name is Llanfairpwllgwyngyllgogerychwyrndrobwllllantysil-iogOGOgoch. It literally means: Saint Mary's Church in the hollow of the white hazel near a rapid whirlpool and the Church of St. Tysilio of the red cave. 'OGO' comes from the word 'ogof' meaning 'cave' in Welsh. A lot of his parishes were to be called St. Mary's funnily enough. His second posting was also in Wales where he was curate at the Church of St. Tegfan's in Llandegfan near Beaumaris from 1913 to 1915.

In 1917 he became a chaplain to the forces but we know little of his time in WWI.

Through the Chaplain's Museum website, Barry Hillier, my researcher from Holyhead, found John C. Lloyd's application card to the Chaplaincy Service. In order to join the forces he would have been interviewed by the Chaplain-General, Bishop John Taylor Smith who was responsible

JOHN COLLINS LLOYD AS A YOUNG CURATE.

JOHN COLLINS LLOYD AS CAPTAIN IN THE ARMY OF THE CHAPLAIN SERVICE IN WWI.

for recruitment for the Church of England. The interview would have taken place at the War Office in London. According to the website, the candidates would have been asked a lot of questions and, of course, needed to pass a medical test. Below is Courtenay Lloyd's father's application:

It's rather nice to read the bishop's final comments at the bottom of the card: 'bright, frank fellow'. Yes, well I think he was both bright and frank, and a very nice chap to use the vocabulary of the era.

Later I found a letter from my grandfather written from The Bonnington Hotel on Southampton Row in London dated 2 April 1917 which must have been the day of his interview. In the letter he tells his fiancée, Dorothy Gertrude Scull, how it went: 'You will of course be anxious to hear how I got on with the Chaplain General this afternoon. I have nothing definite to tell you. The old chap was awfully decent, but inclined to be very pious in his conversation. He asked me all sorts of questions and finally gave me a paper to take to the Medical Board at Chelsea Hospital. I did my best to get him to commit himself one way or another, but he said he could do nothing until he heard from the Medical Board. Eventually, after a good deal of coaxing, I induced him to admit that my case would receive his favourable consideration. I also

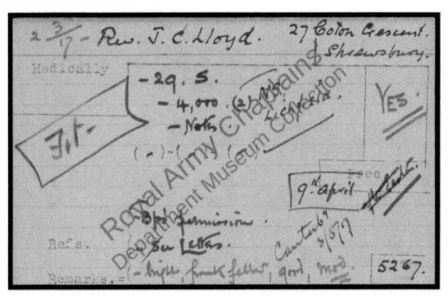

REVD. JOHN COLLINS LLOYD APPROVED APPLICATION CARD TO JOIN
THE ARMY AS CHAPLAIN TO THE FORCES.

caught him writing the two words "after Easter" on the sheet containing my record'. He then goes on to say, 'After leaving him I called at Burberry's to be measured'. I presume he meant to be measured for his chaplain's uniform. The Chaplain-General must have had a good impression of my grandfather otherwise he would probably not have sent him for the medical test. His words 'after Easter' came true as John Collins Lloyd was admitted to the army and became an army chaplain on 3 May 1917. It's wonderful to have his firsthand account of the interview.

I think for history's sake it is fitting to include a photograph of the first page of this letter in this biography.

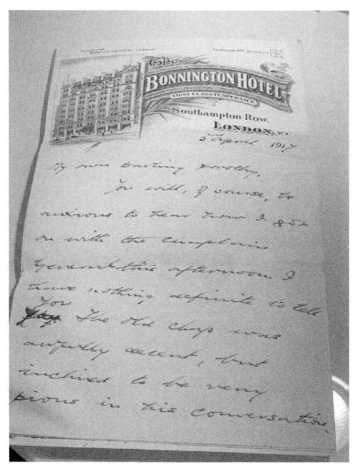

JOHN COLLINS LLOYD'S LETTER DATED 2 APRIL 1917 TO
HIS FIANCÉE ABOUT HIS INTERVIEW WITH THE CHAPLAIN
GENERAL IN LONDON FOR ENTRY INTO THE ARMY
TO BECOME A CHAPLAIN OF THE FORCES.

JOHN COLLINS LLOYD'S PLACE OF
RESIDENCE IN SHREWSBURY.

It's not quite clear how much time he spent in the army or what he did. What we do know though is that from Wales, the church sent him to England, to St. Mary's Church in Shrewsbury in about 1916, a year or so before he became chaplain. There he lived on 27 Coton Crescent. He wasn't very keen on Shrewsbury, complaining to his fiancée of having 'Shrewsburyitis', and told her he missed the sea of his native Anglesey.

It was here that John Collins Lloyd met and fell in love with Dorothy Gertrude Scull. After a beautiful courtship, and I know it was as I have his love letters to her which are always addressed 'my adored Dolly', they married in 1918. For the purpose of finding out more about their era, I read his letters which were written in 1916 and 1917, hoping to glean more information of the times, WWI and the death of his brother Noel in 1916. But I found out very little, apart from the reference to the interview with the Chaplain General, as all he writes is of his passionate love for his 'Dolly'. I felt as though I was intruding on their intimacy but was also very impressed with just how much he loved her. His feelings for her are extraordinary and the way he writes, so touching, so spiritual and so adoring. In the first letters he addresses her as Miss Dorothy Gertrude Scull but that soon changes and she becomes his adored Dolly. On 26 September 1916, he writes, 'Dearest of all. I am sending this little message to greet you when you come down tomorrow morning. Even now I cannot realise that you are my own sweet Dorothy. All I can grasp at present is the fact that your dear people have given me a precious jewel to guard and cherish. I feel so terribly selfish about it, and, oh, so very, very unworthy. I have nothing in the whole world to give you except a great and overpowering love, and that you shall have for ever and ever. What a good thing you cannot see me now! I have a big lump in my throat and the tears are in my eyes as I think about it all. Dorrie, darling, I cannot possibly put my feelings on paper and when I am with you I am speechless. How I wish I could come to you instead of this message and give you a big hug and kiss you over and over again. Goodbye, beloved. Ever your loving John'. Theirs was true love. His capacity for loving is extraordinary. He says he cannot put his feelings on paper but he does it so beautifully. I also felt tears in my eyes as I read the above and the other letters. I cherish them and they will stay in our family forever.

Their courtship was very sweet. I learned from my grandfather's letters that they would often meet on the bridge in Shrewsbury. I suspect the bridge must have been the old English Bridge rather than the Welsh Bridge a bit further out of town as it was nearer where they lived. Both bridges cross the River Severn. They agreed to go by bicycle - what other way to travel for young people in those days? It would have only been a short ride away for both of them as they lived quite near. He also talks about seeing her in Castle Street. We know that her family worshipped at the church where John Collins Lloyd was curate, St. Mary's so maybe that was where they first met.

Their wedding took place in Uphill (near Weston-super-Mare) at The Old Church of St. Nicholas, Somerset on 15 January 1918, and they went on honeymoon to Clevedon. This church was in many ways the Scull's family church.

COURTENAY'S PARENTS' MARRIAGE CERTIFICATE.

After their marriage and once he became a vicar his parishes were: St. Editha's Church, Amington, near Tamworth (County Warwick 1919 - 1920), St. Mary's, Edstaston (Shrewsbury, 1920 - 1924), parish church of St Mary, Sledmere (Yorkshire, previously the East Riding of Yorkshire, 1924 - 1928), St. Mary's Church, Henbury (Bristol, 1928 - 1957). He was the vicar at Henbury for 29 years. He was also appointed rural dean of Almondsbury (near Bristol) on 3 November 1945. He didn't quite make it to bishop but on 1 July 1949 he was made a canon by the Bishop of Bristol. Upon his retirement he became Canon Emeritus of Bristol Cathedral.

In Henbury they lived at the new vicarage built specially for the family as the old vicarage was in a bad state. The new vicarage is located on Station Road, Henbury. Reverend John Collins Lloyd retired to Ickenham (Middlesex) with his wife to live near his daughter Gloria (18 Ivy House Road). They moved into 17 Hoylake Crescent where we would stay nearly every Christmas.

Courtenay's father looks a serious man but actually he was quite an extrovert with a great sense of humour. He used to tease me as a child and I loved it. From stories I gleaned from my father, I gather my grandfather was quite a modern man for his times. As a young curate he rode a bicycle to get around but as soon as he could he invested in a car. Owning a car in the 1920s was not at all common. Not long afterwards he would invest in the latest camera available and it is thanks to this camera that there are so many family photos in our possession.

A 1926 MORRIS COWLEY BULLNOSE CAR.

Courtenay remembers the first car his father bought. He says it was in Sledmere and even remembers the make and model: a Morris Cowley Bullnose. I showed my father a picture of a similar car and he said, 'Oh, yes, that's it!' It must have been about 1926, and judging by the photograph it was a beautiful motor car.

I asked him what his reaction was to his father buying this car. He told me that as he was a young boy of about seven, he found it very exciting. He also told me the family would 'motor' to nearby Scarborough and Bridlington in it. I wondered how his father, a vicar, could possibly have afforded it. My father thinks he paid for it out of his salary. I also asked how his father learned to drive or pass his test. But of course there was no driving test in the 1920s. I think it only came into force in the mid 1930s. He told me that a man from a local garage taught his father to drive. No doubt my grandfather far preferred visiting his parishioners in his fancy new car rather than on a bicycle. There is a photo of my father and his brother Raymond as little boys next to a car with his father at the wheel, and his mother and another lady in the back seats. He thinks it was taken in Sledmere but is not sure whether the car in the photo is the Morris Cowley.

MY FATHER AND SOME MEMBERS OF HIS FAMILY
IN A CAR IN SLEDMERE IN ABOUT 1926.

John Collins Lloyd must have been a very organized person too. I know because his parish church appointment documents which I now have in my possession are still in immaculate order. He also invested his money carefully and when he died he had quite a number of shares in popular companies of the times. Unfortunately when my father tried to cash them in it was a little too late as many of the companies no longer existed.

He read the newspapers too as my father always has but according to him, my grandfather did not read a 'posh paper like *The Times*' but the *Daily Mail* which he said was a very popular paper at the time although in later years he would subscribe to *The Daily Telegraph* just as my father does today. He also told me his father always voted Conservative which of course my father did too.

When my mother met him for the first time, she took to her future father-in-law immediately and the feeling was mutual. They both had sharp minds as well as a great sense of humour. I remember him as a wonderful grandfather even though I was only four when he died.

He led a quiet life during his retirement with his adored Dorothy, and with his daughter Gloria and her family nearby. I remember when we stayed with them, after meals my grandmother would wash up and he would do the drying in perfect tandem. He would go for walks in the afternoons and called them his 'constitutional' which I suppose was the word they used in those days. On one of those walks, he fell but got up again and feeling perfectly well, walked home. However the fall caused a blood clot which was not detected until quite a while later when it was too late. Revd. Canon John Collins Lloyd, Courtenay's father, died on 19 March 1961 in Uxbridge. I was very small but remember the phone call when we lived in Ruskington. What a shock it was.

My father took the news as he always does, calm on the outside but no doubt, infinitely sad on the inside. After all, his father was only 74, far too young to die. Below the clipping announcing his death from the *Western Daily Press* dated 4 April 1961.

DEATH OF CANON LLOYD

Western Daily Press Reporter

Canon John Collins Lloyd, who saw Henbury transformed from a quiet village to a thriving Bristol suburb during his 29 years as vicar there, has died at Ickenham, Middlesex.

He had been living at Ickenham, latterly, since his retirement as vicar of Henbury in May, 1957.

Canon Lloyd, who at one time was also Rural Dean of Almondsbury, was nominated to an honorary canonry in Bristol Cathedral by the Bishop in 1949.

He later became a Canon Emeritus of Bristol Cathedral.

Gift

Formerly at Sledmore, Malton, in Yorkshire, he was inducted as vicar of Henbury with Aust and Northwick in 1928.

When Canon Lloyd retired, over 270 parishioners attended a farewell party and he was presented with a cheque for £571.

He leaves a widow, a son and a daughter.

The funeral service will be at Ickenham tomorrow.

TV show softens the blow

Bristol Youth Choir night met their first o nents in the national of the B.B.C.'s "Let People Sing" competiti and lost.

Home Service listeners them defeated by Hull O Junior Choir.

But the Bristol regional winners in the c youth choirs class, have vision date ahead.

They have been inv! the Bristol Youth Orch

CLIPPING ANNOUNCING THE DEATH OF
COURTENAY'S FATHER CANON
JOHN COLLINS LLOYD.

My father didn't remember where his father was buried. In our research we were happy to learn he was with his son, Raymond, at the same church where he got married, The Old Church of St. Nicholas of Uphill near Weston-super-Mare. We also suspect my grandmother, Dorothy Gertrude Scull, is there too.

JOHN COLLINS LLOYD'S SIBLINGS

John Collins Lloyd, Courtenay's father, was the eldest of five siblings; William, Ellen, Tom and Owen Noel. The former were always referred to by my father as: 'Uncle Will', 'Aunty Nell' and 'Uncle Tom'. Owen Noel Lloyd was never mentioned. While researching for this biography, we found he died very young.

COURTENAY'S FATHER JOHN COLLINS LLOYD
WITH HIS NEXT SIBLING DOWN, WILLIAM FOX
LLOYD (UNCLE WILL) IN HOLYHEAD
IN THEIR CHILDHOOD.

UNCLE WILL
(William Fox Lloyd 1890 - 1973)

Worked for the Clyde Valley Company. He married 'Aunty Gwen' (Gwendoline Price Hughes 1890 - 1970) in Dennistoun, Larnarkshire, Scotland in 1917. They had two daughters and one son: Gwendoline (Gwen), Blodwen and William Evan who was known as Gwyllim in the family and who became a doctor. His daughter, Katriona Fox Lloyd tells me they spoke Welsh at home.

These cousins, with very Welsh names, lived in Scotland but there was hardly any contact with that branch of the family. In our research for this book we miraculously found them. The help of Katriona Fox Lloyd, William Fox Lloyd junior's granddaughter, was invaluable when she gave me information about the family in Scotland. She also provided me with old photos of her grandfather, Uncle Will, his family and even photos of my father and his family, photos we had never seen before.

COURTENAY'S PATERNAL UNCLE,
WILLIAM FOX LLOYD.

UNCLE WILLIAM AND AUNTY GWEN'S CHILDREN – MY FATHER'S FIRST COUSINS FROM GLASGOW

As children, these cousins were close, meeting in the summer on the beach in North Wales. Below is a photo of Raymond with his cousins William Evan Fox Lloyd and Blodwen Fox Lloyd. Blodwen is on a horse which Raymond is leading and William Evan is behind her. What a find, what a lovely photo! Isn't it funny to see how young boys wore ties in that era and even on the beach? Blodwen looks like a free spirit for those rather rigid times with her lovely smile and carefree look.

From Katriona and another family tree on Ancestry.com, we learned that Blodwen had married James Murray and that they had a daughter called Pamela Murray. Gwendoline had a son with Norman Woolstenhulme called Lloyd Woolstenhulme. Their younger brother, William Evan Fox Lloyd married Katriona Ishbel MacLeod (1921-2001) and their daughter is Katriona Fox Lloyd, my second cousin who we discovered in our research. Katriona is married to Paul Mallon and they have a son called Jack Fox Lloyd Mallon.

RIGHT TO LEFT, RAYMOND IN GLASSES, BLODWEN AND LITTLE WILLIAM IN NORTH WALES IN THE EARLY TO MID 1930s.

AUNTY GWEN
FROM GLASGOW -
GWENDOLINE PRICE
HUGHES.

BLODWEN PRICE
LLOYD (1918 - 1964).

GWENDOLINE
ELIZABETH FOX
LLOYD (1921 - 1990).

WILLIAM EVAN FOX LLOYD DR. (1925 - 1993).

AUNTY NELL/NELLIE
(Ellen Lloyd 1893 - 1988)

Aunty Nell, who lived to the ripe old age of 95 and outlived all her siblings, married a man called Tom Breese and they later lived in a small town called Valley in Anglesey. My father remembers their daughter, Mona, his cousin, very well. Mona died in Morecambe in 2012 but her daughter Jennifer Lloyd Radford is alive and living in the Lake District. While writing this biography, she seemed to be the last missing piece in the puzzle of my father's family tree but we found her and now the tree is complete.

ELLEN (NELL) LLOYD - MY FATHER'S AUNT
WITH HER DAUGHTER MONA.

Jennifer's godmother is Aunty Peggy, the wife of Uncle Tom, my father's godfather. Jennifer knew them very well. She told me she had visited him a few times on his ship which was berthed in Liverpool after his 'regular voyages as Master on the Calcutta run'. She has quite a few mementoes of his travels to India in her house. My father has too; a pair of carved wooden elephants to hold up his books. I have always seen them on his bookshelves and shall treasure them now I know they were from his Uncle Tom. Jennifer also remembers Uncle Will and Aunty Gwen coming to see her 'Nain' and 'Daid' in Four Mile Bridge in Wales, from Glasgow. She and her mother Mona were also close to my father's sister Gloria. She told me about a holiday with Gloria, her husband Derek and their children, my cousins, Jacqueline, Michael and Antony, spent in Four Mile Bridge in 1966. She said they had happy times on a beach at Rhosneigr with her corgi and that it was a terrible shock when they were all killed on a flight to Yugoslavia 5 years later. It was so good to make contact with Jennifer, or Jenny, as she is called, my newly found cousin.

Soon after my parents were married, Courtenay took Elena to visit North Wales and they called on Aunty Nell. Aunty Nell's wedding present to them was a set of glasses we still have here at home in Madrid. From there he took his new wife to Mount Snowdon by train which he climbed on foot and down again, of course. She took the train both ways. He chuckled when he told me this. He was the walker, my mother never was. Once when my daughter Olivia was very little, she asked her, 'Grandma, why don't you go for walks like Grandpa', to which she answered, 'Oh, I walk a lot in the kitchen!'

UNCLE TOM
(Tom Fox Lloyd 1897 - 1971)

UNCLE TOM AND AUNTY PEGGY
ON THEIR WEDDING DAY.

Uncle Tom was my father's godfather. My father didn't remember that but I found a tiny little leather bound Book of Common Prayer with an inscription inside saying: 'To Charles Courtenay Lloyd from his godfather T. Fox Lloyd 24th May 1919'. His uncle was with the Merchant Navy and his elder brother, John, was always worried he would die in WWI. One of his ships was torpedoed by a U-boat but he survived. Apparently for British merchant ships in WWI and in WWII there was nothing more terrible than the German submarines. I heard later that he was right to be worried as more than 500 ships were known to be sunk in the Irish Sea by U-boats during the war. Uncle Tom married a woman my father remembers fondly, Aunty Peggy. Maybe she was his godmother? I like to think she was.

Upon retirement they went to live in Worthing so that Uncle Tom 'could see his ships go by' (my father's words). On the back of a grainy old photo with Courtenay and Raymond, dated 1928 my father wrote, 'for decades an officer, later Captain in the Merchant Navy'.

They had no children and both died in Worthing.

COURTENAY AND HIS YOUNGER BROTHER RAYMOND
IN JUNE 1928 WITH THEIR UNCLE TOM.

OWEN NOEL LLOYD
Christmas Day 1899 *to* 24 *October* 1916

Arholiad y Bwrdd Canol

YN YSGOLION SIROL MON.

Pasiodd y rhai isod arholiad blynyddol y Bwrdd:—

CAERGYBI.

HONOURS CERTIFICATE.

Arтом Evans: Additional mathematics, physics, chemistry, geography (senior).
Fanny Pollocoff: Additional mathematics,* physics, chemistry, geography (senior).

HIGHER CERTIFICATE.

John Jones: History, Latin, additional mathematics.
Louie Morris: Additional mathematics, physics, chemistry, Latin (senior).
Rice Williams: Additional mathematics, physics, chemistry.

SENIOR CERTIFICATE.

Catherine Abbit: E., A., P†, Ph.
A. R. Breese: H., A., M., W., Ch.
A. T. Fernley: E., H., A., M., F., Ch, G.
Cecil E. Gregory: E., H., A.*, M., F.*†, Ph., Ch.*, G.
Kathleen Isherwood: E., A., M., F., Ch., G.
Ellen H. Jones: E., H., A., L., W., Ch., G.
Lilly Jones: E., A., M., W., Ch.
R. O. Jones: H., A., M., W., Ph.
H. H. Owen: E., H., A., M., W., Ph., Ch.
Olwen Shaw: E., H., A., M., P†, G.
Estella Slater: E., H., A., F†, Ch.
H. O. Williams: E., H., A., W., Ph.
Roger J. Williams: E., H., A., W.

JUNIOR CERTIFICATE.

J. O. Edwards: E., H., A., M., F., Ch.
M. Blodwen Hughes: E., H.*, A.*, M.*, L., F.†, Ph., Ch.*
Iorwerth Jones: E., H., A., M., W.*, Ch.*, Ph.
Ll. Madoc Jones: E., H., A.*, M.*, L., W.*, Ph., Ch.*
R. H. Jones: E., H., A.*, W.*, Ch.*
Noel Lloyd: E., A., M., F†, Ph., Ch
Caroline Lockде: E., H., A., M., L., W., Ch.
Malcolm Riley: E., H., A.* M., F.†, Ph., Ch.
Geoffrey Roberts: E., A., M., Ph., Ch.*
Alex. Stirrat: E., A.*, M., Ph., Ch.*
Nellie Williams, V.: E., H., A., W., Ch.
M. Blodwen Williams: E., H., A.*, M., W.*, Ph., Ch.*
Madge Williams: E.*, H.*, A.*, M., F.†, Ch.*

E., English Language and Literature; H., History; A., Arithmetic; M., Elementary Mathematics; L., Latin; W., Welsh; F., French; Ph., Physics; Ch., Chemistry; G., Geography; *, With distinction; †, With conversational power.

OWEN NOEL LLOYD'S JUNIOR
SCHOOL CERTIFICATE.

Mysteriously, in another Lloyd family tree on Ancestry.com during our research for this book, we found a fifth sibling for Courtenay's father. Many documents pointed to his existence. The funny thing was that my father couldn't remember him. Later he would.

It was Barry Hillier from Holyhead who provided me with some interesting information about Noel. From an old cutting from the local paper at the time, "Yr Herald Cymraeg", and dated 15 September 1908, we can see that Noel passed his Junior Certificate at his school, Holyhead Grammar School. He got a distinction in French. Being good at languages seems to run in the family.

Like his older brothers, Noel attended Sunday school at the church of St. Cybi's, the family church. Here he would have learned Welsh and it was also here that his funeral would have taken place. It was Barry Hillier who found his burial certificate which would confirm his early death.

Owen Noel had died of TB aged just 16. My grandfather, John Collins Lloyd was the informant and it seems a very sad coincidence that he should lose both a brother and a son aged 16.

BURIALS in the Parish of _Holyhead_ _in the County of_ _Anglesey_ _in the year One thousand eight hundred and_ _Sixteen_

Name.	Abode.	When Buried.	Age.	By whom the Ceremony was performed.
Owen Noel Lloyd. No. 1641	19 Alderley Terrace, Holyhead	Oct. 27th 1916.	16	Evan Thomas (Curate)

THE BURIAL CERTIFICATE OF MY FATHER'S YOUNGEST PATERNAL UNCLE, OWEN NOEL LLOYD.

His grave is in the civil part of the Maeshhyfryd cemetery in Holyhead. He lies next to his parents, William Fox Lloyd senior and Marian Margaret Collins. The inscription for Noel has faded badly but on closer inspection you can just make out the following: 'In loving memory of Noel. Beloved youngest son of William and Marian Fox Lloyd, Alderley Terrace. Born Christmas Day 1899. Died 24th October 1916. On the base we think it says, 'Thy will be done'. How sad. So he was born on Christmas Day 1899, hence his lovely name, Noel. This is his grave.

OWEN NOEL'S GRAVE IN HOLYHEAD.

When I showed the certificate to my father, his memory clicked. He said, 'Oh Noel!' - and not Owen which is what I thought the boy was called as it was his first name. No wonder he didn't know who I was talking about when I asked him about his Uncle Owen and not his Uncle Noel. He then said, 'My father used to mention him'. I'm sure he did. I felt so sorry about the sad ending of this young boy's life and wished I had a photograph. My wish came true when I made contact with Katriona, Uncle Will's granddaughter. She had a photo of Noel aged 13 and here he is. On the back of it, Noel had written, poignantly, 'with love from Noel'. I wonder who he sent it to? Maybe to his Uncle Will as Katriona has the picture and Uncle Will was her grandfather.

NOEL OWEN LLOYD -JOHN COLLINS LLOYD'S
YOUNGEST BROTHER 1899 - 1916.

***'UNCLE DAVID', DAVID JOHN COLLINS. SURVEYOR DURING THE BRITISH EMPIRE IN INDIA, BURMA AND SIAM

Born Stirling Scotland in 1854 and son of John Collins who was with the 82nd Regiment of Foot (1827 - 1904). Married Elian Emily Collins née Pemberton at Moulmein, Bengal, India. Employed as a surveyor. Died Bangkok (Thailand) 1912.

My father always used to talk about a certain Uncle David who had lived in Thailand but I didn't know who he was. It was quite obvious the Collins middle name must have come from my grandfather's mother's side whose name my father couldn't remember either. That was when my friend and researcher and genealogist for this book, Andrew Dale, helped. He started doing a family tree for the Lloyd side of my father's family on www.ancestry.com.

Andrew Dale found my father's paternal grandmother via the site and she was Marian Margaret Collins who was born in the British Raj, in Delhi in 1860 and was the daughter of John Collins. Well, it turns out that the David John Collins we were looking for was indeed her brother. Thus he is my father's great uncle.

My father had told me 'Uncle David' had been given some medal from the King of Siam (now Thailand). He was apparently awarded the medals for important surveying works he carried out there. I never really listened and wasn't really interested. However, when going through old documents and letters for this biography, I came across a file with a note written by my paternal grandmother that said, 'Uncle David's White Elephant Medals'. Inside were some amazing, elaborately hand painted, and very official looking old scrolls which looked like they were from

Thailand. When I asked my father for further information he could no longer remember. There was even a medal.

ONE OF UNCLE DAVID'S WHITE ELEPHANT
INSIGNIAS AND MEDALS FROM THE
KING OF SIAM IN 1897.

When I examined the papers I saw that 'Uncle David' had been awarded the Insignia of the Order of the Crown of Siam of the Third Class as well as the Insignia of the White Elephant of the Fourth Class. Both were conferred by King Mongkut of Siam in 1897 and are signed by him. The scrolls are hand painted as are the envelopes. Then there is a letter to my great uncle from the ambassador in Bangkok. It was from George Greville KCMG who refers to himself as 'HMM' (Her Majesty's Minister) and dated 24 August 1897 to authorize the recipient to accept and wear them.

This is a letter the ambassador sent 'upon instructions from Lord Salisbury' who was the prime minister at the time and during the reign of Queen Victoria. It begins, 'Sir, with reference to your letter to Mr. Archer of the 9th April last, and in accordance with instructions from Lord Salisbury, I transmit to you herewith, Her Majesty's License authorizing you to accept and wear the Insignia of the Order of the "White Elephant" of the 4th Class and the Order of Siam, of the 3rd Class, conferred upon you by the King of Siam. I am, Sir, your obedient servant, HMM Resident George Greville.'

The letter attaches the licence from 'The Court of King James' to allow the recipient to wear the orders and includes a handwritten paragraph explaining the insignias: 'His Majesty the King of Siam has been pleased to confer upon you the Insignia of the Order of the Crown of Siam of the Third Class in recognition of your services while actually and entirely

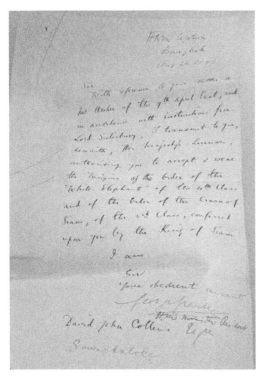

LETTER FROM THE AMBASSADOR
TO 'UNCLE DAVID'.

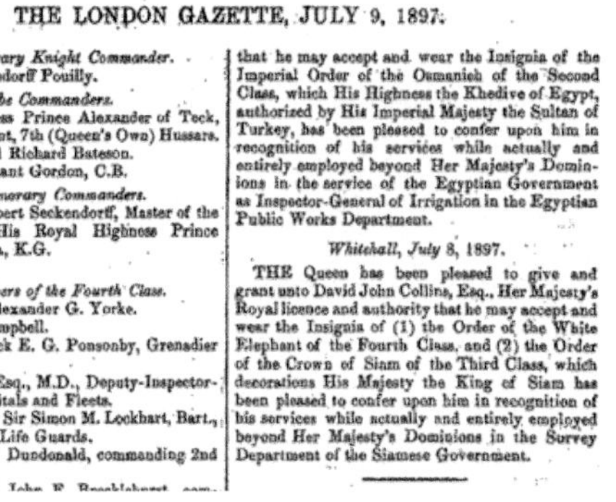

THE LONDON GAZETTE, JULY 9, 1897.

orary *Knight Commander.*
nsdorff Pouilly.
to be Commanders.
ness Prince Alexander of Teck,
ant, 7th (Queen's Own) Hussars.
al Richard Bateson.
Grant Gordon, C.B.
Honorary Commanders.
Albert Seckendorff, Master of the
His Royal Highness Prince
nia, K.G.

mbers of the Fourth Class.
Alexander G. Yorke.
ampbell.
rick E. G. Ponsonby, Grenadier

Esq., M.D., Deputy-Inspector-
pitals and Fleets.
el Sir Simon M. Lockhart, Bart.,
t Life Guards.
of Dundonald, commanding 2nd

that he may accept and wear the Insignia of the Imperial Order of the Osmanieh of the Second Class, which His Highness the Khedive of Egypt, authorized by His Imperial Majesty the Sultan of Turkey, has been pleased to confer upon him in recognition of his services while actually and entirely employed beyond Her Majesty's Dominions in the service of the Egyptian Government as Inspector-General of Irrigation in the Egyptian Public Works Department.

Whitehall, July 8, 1897.

THE Queen has been pleased to give and grant unto David John Collins, Esq., Her Majesty's Royal licence and authority that he may accept and wear the Insignia of (1) the Order of the White Elephant of the Fourth Class, and (2) the Order of the Crown of Siam of the Third Class, which decorations His Majesty the King of Siam has been pleased to confer upon him in recognition of his services while actually and entirely employed beyond Her Majesty's Dominions in the Survey Department of the Siamese Government.

THE ANNOUNCEMENT OF THE WHITE ELEPHANT MEDALS FROM THE KING OF SIAM IN 1897 AWARDED TO MY FATHER'S GREAT UNCLE DAVID JOHN COLLINS.

employed beyond Our Dominions in the Survey Department of the Siamese Government'.

Andrew also found a clipping of the announcement that Queen Victoria had given him permission to accept and wear the White Elephant order medals. Here is the clipping that makes this story come true. It's from The London Gazette and is dated 9 July 1897. What a find.

Andrew Dale also found David John Collins's grave in the Protestant Cemetery in Bangkok lovingly placed there by his wife Emily.

From our unofficial researcher, Barry Hillier, we received the records of his marriage to Emily Pemberton. From them we could see they married in Burma. I wondered what he was doing there as I had assumed all his surveying work was in Thailand. On the same record, under his name were the intriguing letters 'G.T. Survey'. Google provided the answer. Uncle David had worked for the 'Great Trigonometrical Survey' in India. This included the measurement of the height of the Himalayan Mountains, Everest, K2 and Kanchenjunga. I also wondered who his bride was.

UNCLE DAVID'S GRAVE IN THE PROTESTANT CEMETERY IN BANGKOK.

DAVID JOHN COLLINS'S WIFE, AUNTY EMILY: ELIAN EMILY COLLINS NÉE PEMBERTON 1858 - 1945 – EMINENT BOTANIST AND MBE

Among my father's old family papers and photographs I finally discovered that the mysterious lady sitting in a drawing room was Emily Pemberton, David John Collin's wife. I hadn't thought to look on the back of the photo where my father wrote the following: 'Aunty Emily in her drawing room in Bangkok. She was half Burmese, I think, and married to my paternal grandmother's brother David John Collins'.

There was also a beautiful postcard of the house itself called, unsurprisingly, 'Collinston' which is on, or rather was on Sarthorn Road in Bangkok. Sadly, today, it no longer exists.

EMILY PEMBERTON, DAVID JOHN COLLINS'S WIFE IN THEIR TOWN HOUSE IN BANGKOK. SHE IS WEARING HER MBE MEDAL.

CollinsOn" Sarthorn Road. Bangkok. Siam.

DAVID J. COLLINS AND EMILY PEMBERTON'S
TOWN HOUSE IN BANGKOK.

I must say my father's notes on the back of photos have turned out to be very useful in documenting the history of his family. On the back of this photo my father had written: 'Uncle David's town house in Bangkok. Aunty (Emily Pemberton) left it in her will to the British Government. It is now British Embassy in Bangkok'. My father told me that his father had always said that Emily was rather rich. When, during research for this book, I finally made contact with my cousin Katriona Fox Lloyd in Scotland, she knew a little bit more about Elian Emily Collins née Pemberton. It seems she was an eminence in herself.

Emily Pemberton was born in Burma. Her father was Colonel William Walker George Pemberton who at the time was deputy commissioner with British Burma. Later he was with the Madras Staff Corps in India. Born in Quebec on 26 November 1835 I was curious to see who his wife was or rather who was Emily's mother? Was my father right when he said his Aunty Emily was half Burmese? From our research we found out he had married Adèle Isabelle Sandfield Macdonald in Kensington, London in 1874. They had six children none of which was named Emily.

It was Karen Stapley, curator for the East India Company Records from the British Library, who would find out for us. After consulting the records, she wrote to say: 'We have a baptism entry for Emily Pemberton which states that she was born 4 September 1858 and baptised in Moulmein 12 April 1865. It gives her parents as W W Pemberton and "a Burmese woman named Ma-Miggaley". From the way in which the baptism entry is written and the fact I have not been able to find a marriage entry I would assume they were unmarried. It was not that uncommon for officials in India and Burma to have a local wife, however, unless the wife converted to Christianity there tends to be no record of their marriage and local marriage that may have taken place was not recognised as legally binding by the British government.' How bigoted society was in those days.

So, finally we knew that Aunty Emily's mother was indeed Burmese as my father had thought. Thanks to the British Library in London we now know her name was Ma-Miggaley. Despite not being married to Emily's mother, her father took good care of her education and it's thanks to this she would later become an eminent botanist.

Who would have thought that with those beginnings, Elian Emily Collins née Pemberton would become a big name in botany, be awarded an MBE and turn out to be our most illustrious ancestor? I am delighted for her but I do wish we knew more about her mother. What a story.

Emily married David John Collins on 25 June 1877 in her native Maulmain, Burma. She travelled with him when his surveying work took him to India and to Thailand where she would later live until her death in 1945. They had two daughters. Ellen Marion Collins was their firstborn arriving one year after their marriage. Born in Maulmain in 1878, Ellen Marion married Basil Edwin Le Blond Holloway (1874 - 1939) in Ticehurst, East Sussex on 5 September 1901. Sadly she died, aged only 25, on 13 September 1903 in Leigh (Kent). Aunty Emily and Uncle David's other child, Emily Pemberton Collins was born in 1880 in Darjeeling but did not live more than one month. This must have been when her husband was working for the Trigonometric Survey of India. Emily's husband died in 1912 but she lived on until 1945. She buried him at the Protestant Cemetery in Bangkok. I think she lies there with him too. It must have been a huge blow for her to lose her children so early and then her husband aged only 58.

She would become a big name in botany, finding species in Thailand and exporting them to fellow botanists and gardens all over the world. I can only imagine that she found solace in this field and perhaps also among the large British community in former Siam.

Emily was also a naturalist and would become one of the first members of The Natural History Society of Siam when it was established on 6 March 1914. It was thanks to her that the mosquito eating fish, the Gamusia, was released into Thai waters in 1929.

She frequently sent specimens to the Royal Botanic Gardens at Kew. Emily Pemberton corresponded with Sir Arthur William Hill the director of the RBG at the time. Some of the specimens can be seen in the Natural History Museum in London. Several plant species have the term 'collinsae' or 'collinsiae' in their name in her honour. Indeed what an honour. The Argyreia Collinsae (Na Songhkla) is just one example.

PLANT ARGYREIA COLLINSAE (NA SONGHKLA).

As the doyenne of the British residents in Bangkok and for her contributions to botany, 'Aunty Emily' was awarded an MBE (Member of the Order of the British Empire) in the King's Birthday Honours List of 1938.

This makes her our most illustrious ancestor together with Uncle David. As she outlived all her family she left her estate to the British government. Her town house, Collinston, was bequeathed to the British government and became for a while the British Embassy. What a pity the building no longer exists.

I am curious to know how her photo, the photo of her house, and the medal and medal scrolls of her husband, 'Uncle David', somehow ended up in my house near Madrid. I can only imagine he, or she, sent them to my grandfather at some time. I have my father to thank for keeping them for all these years. They shall be well looked after.

COURTENAY'S MOTHER
DOROTHY GERTRUDE SCULL
AND HER SISTER GWENDOLINE

Dorothy Gertrude Scull (born Attingham, Atcham, Shrewsbury 31 October 1892, died 27 December 1970, aged 79, in Ickenham). Daughter of Charles Edward Scull from Abbey Foregate, Shrewsbury and Bessy Elizabeth Walters.

She had one younger sister, Gwendoline Scull who married Harold Benson.

They had a daughter, Angela, born on 19 August 1924. He was a lieutenant in the Royal Field Engineers and earned a Silver War Badge (discharged on account of ill health).

GWENDOLINE SCULL
AND HAROLD BENSON ON
THEIR WEDDING DAY,
JUNE 1923 EDSTASTON.

HAROLD BENSON,
GWENDOLINE'S FIRST
HUSBAND, IN HIS
WWI UNIFORM.

WALTER WILLIAMS,
GWENDOLINE'S SECOND
HUSBAND.

Harold Benson died in 1927 from wounds sustained in WWI and Gwendoline remarried. My father remembers his mother crying when she heard. It was such a tragedy as he was so young, just 34 and his daughter Angela a toddler aged three.

Her second husband was called Walter Williams and they married in 1929 in Pontypool. Both Gwendoline, my father's aunt, and her daughter, Angela, his cousin, would live in Wales forever afterwards.

My father remembers their farm in Greenmeadow in Cwmbran, Monmouthsire, Wales.

It was a working farm for 250 years, dating back to 1752. My father describes the beautiful green fields with cows and horses and how he saw Angela milking cows or riding on a tractor with her stepfather. When Gwendoline died, Angela Benson continued to look after her stepfather Walter Williams until his death. Later Angela moved to Newport. During research for this book, we found out that Angela is still alive and living in Cwmbran in Wales.

Angela and my father were very close cousins and had for many years exchanged Christmas cards until they lost contact. Now, that we have found her again, he also has a hundredth birthday card from his only long-lost cousin on his mother's side to add to his collection.

GREENMEADOW FARM.

MY FATHER'S COUSIN ANGELA AND HER DOG *TASS*
ON THE FAMILY FARM, GREENMEADOW IN 1970.

When George and I were children, 'Aunty Angela' unfailingly sent us birthday and Christmas presents. We had to send her thank you letters which were always addressed to her and her stepfather, known to us as 'Uncle Walter'. They ran this farm in Wales and it must have been a hard life. I never met her but my mother did when my parents made a special trip to visit her after their retirement. I am told that up until a short while ago - now she is living in a care home - she lived as in days gone by with no fridge, no washing machine and no central heating. She is apparently a tiny little woman who weighs only five stone. That doesn't surprise me as her Aunty Dorothy, my father's mother, was a tiny woman too. My brother got his height (over 6ft) from his father and grandfather, and I got my short stature (5ft 4in.) from my grandmother.

In 1901, Dorothy or Dolly, as her husband John Collins Lloyd called her, and her family, including her sister, Gwendoline, Angela's mother, were living at 31 Castle St, Shrewsbury. It is a beautiful old Tudor building.

Courtenay's mother was an accomplished pianist and I have her diploma, dated Christmas 1916 qualifying her as a Licentiate of the Royal Academy of Music (LRAM), hanging in its original frame above her beautiful old piano. Although this qualified her to teach she only ever played the piano for pleasure. The piano has remained in the family ever since, having been played by her daughter Gloria and granddaughter Jacqueline as well as my dear brother George. Today it stands sadly in our lounge at home with no one to play it but is a beautiful memory of bygone times.

COURTENAY'S MOTHER'S FAMILY HOME AT 31 CASTLE STREET, SHREWSBURY, IN 1901 ACCORDING TO THE CENSUS.

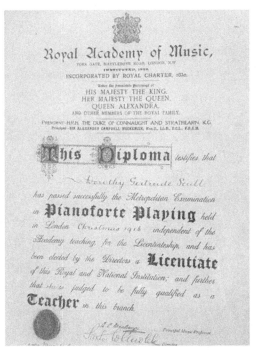

COURTENAY'S MOTHER, DOROTHY GERTRUDE SCULL'S R.A.M. PIANO DIPLOMA DATED 1916.

My grandmother who doted on my father was the person who was the heart of our Christmases when I was a child from a very early age. I have continued her festive traditions until this day. When George and I were children, she would give us exciting stockings to open which were placed at the end of our beds on Christmas morning. Now in their 30s my girls still get a stocking every year. Present opening time was magic and took place after breakfast where the parcels were all lined up under the tree. One year my grandmother gave George Raymond's train set, something she must have treasured for many years after her son's death. I remember her also surreptitiously giving my father a few notes of money which might have been 50 pounds which seemed an enormous amount to me. I have also continued her birthday traditions. As children she would send us a birthday card with a pound note in it and a cake for us both. A pound in the late 60's went an awful long way.

My grandmother also bought my father clothes for his birthday or at Christmas. He probably needed them as he never bought new clothes himself and neither did my mother. Only in later years, when my mother got into knitting when she bought a modern electric knitting machine did she clothe him. He wore her colourful knitted cardigans until they were threadbare out of loyalty to her although they were a bit quaint on him. When he came to live with us in Madrid, I quietly removed them and took him to the big Spanish department store, El Corte Inglés, to kit him out with smart clothing. In my house and in Spain my father had to be well dressed in my opinion. I'm sure my grandmother would have approved.

HIS MATERNAL GRANDFATHER
CHARLES EDWARD SCULL

DOROTHY'S PARENT'S HOUSE WHERE THEY LIVED JUST AFTER THEY GOT MARRIED. 18 BROOK STREET, SHREWSBURY.

Charles Edward Scull (born Bristol 1962, died Shrewsbury 1921) married Elizabeth (Bessy) Walters. Soon after they married they lived at 18 Brook Street, Shrewsbury.

Charles Edward Scull was a contracting engineer. At least that is what it says on his daughter's marriage certificate. Later when Andrew Dale researched the family's history he found him registered in a census as a sanitation and heating engineer. My father told me they were 'business people'. They owned a large laundry called Salop Steam Laundry, on Sutton Road, Shrewsbury which is now a museum.

Once, apparently, they were paid in valuable furniture, some of which were prize pieces that I have inherited and grace our home today. I would never dream of parting with them. They were pretty well off and in 1911 lived at 121 Abbey Foregate, Shrewsbury which was a wealthy area. The house they lived in was very large and no doubt the furniture they were given in lieu of payment would have fitted in easily.

A SALOP STEAM LAUNDRY VAN. THE COMPANY WAS OWNED BY
COURTENAY'S MATERNAL GRANDPARENTS.

THE HOUSE WHERE COURTENAY'S MOTHER AND GRANDPARENTS
LIVED IN ABBEY FOREGATE.

HIS MATERNAL GRANDMOTHER, BESSY (ELIZABETH) GWENDOLINE NÉE WALTERS

My father's maternal grandmother was called Bessy (Elizabeth) Gwendoline Scull née Elizabeth Walters. She was born in Redwick, Montgomeryshire, Wales in about 1868 and married Charles Edward Scull in 1890. It's funny how the two sides of the family are of Welsh origin. She died in Henbury in 1943. In her probate she left more than £10,000 to her two daughters. Her last years were spent living in her splendid house in Weston-super-Mare where her grandchildren spent many a happy summer with her.

COURTENAY'S MATERNAL
GRANDPARENTS, CHARLES EDWARD
SCULL AND ELIZABETH (BESSIE)
WALTERS. ABOUT 1905.

JOHN COLLINS LLOYD AND
DOROTHY GERTRUDE SCULL'S CHILDREN

Charles Courtenay Lloyd born Amington near Tamworth (formerly Country Warwick, Staffordshire today) 1 May 1919.

Married Elena von Lieven (born Rome 7 June 1920, died Bradford 1 October 1999). Married 22 December 1953, Henbury, Bristol.

CHARLES COURTENAY'S LLOYD'S BIRTH CERTIFICATE.

COURTENAY AND ELENA'S CHILDREN

PHOTO OF MASHA AND HER FAMILY IN MADRID
(OLIVIA THEIR YOUNGEST DAUGHTER BACK
ROW (LONG HAIR), SUSANA (SUZY) THEIR
OLDEST DAUGHTER BACK ROW SHORT HAIR).

George Lloyd (born Cambridge 12 February 1955, died London 15 May 2001). Married Sanya Lloyd née Jancic (born Belgrade). She died on 17 October 2008 also in London. No children.

Masha (Maria) Lloyd (born Cambridge 8 February 1957). Lives in Madrid. Masha married Eladio Freijo Calzada (born Montrondo 23 September 1944) in Madrid on 21 August 1983.

ELADIO FREIJO CALZADA,
MASHA'S HUSBAND.

MASHA AND ELADIO'S CHILDREN

MIGUEL ANGEL GARCÍA
BERMEJO (OLIVIA'S
PARTNER).

Susana (Suzy) Freijo Lloyd born Madrid 28 April 1984

Olivia Freijo Lloyd born Madrid 22 May 1985

Olivia Freijo Lloyd's partner. Miguel Angel García Bermejo born Madrid 1975

At the time of writing this biography Olivia was pregnant and her baby boy, Elliot, was born in September 2019. We welcomed a new member into the family and at the same time Courtenay became a very happy and proud great grandfather.

SUSANA (SUZY) FREIJO LLOYD.

OLIVIA FREIJO LLOYD.

CHARLES COURTENAY LLOYD'S SIBLINGS

THE GRAVE OF RAYMOND WILLIAM LLOYD, MY FATHER'S BROTHER WHO DIED TOO YOUNG, AGED JUST 16. HIS FATHER IS BURIED WITH HIM.

Raymond William Lloyd born 5 August 1922 in Edstaton Shrewsbury. Died of infantile paralysis (polio) aged 16 on 15 October 1938 in Weston-super-Mare. The funeral took place at his father's church, St. Mary's of Henbury. Interment took place at The Old Church St. Nicholas, Uphill where his parents got married. It was, I think, the church Courtenay's grandmother, Bessy Scull, and her family attended when in Weston. Thanks to Andrew Dale's discoveries I was very happy to receive a photo of Raymond's grave and to see that his father, John Collins Lloyd was buried with him too. We suspect his mother is also buried there and are still waiting for proof. I had long wondered where they were buried and it is thanks to research for this book that I now know where they are. In the summer of 2019 I visited the grave at the lovely little church near Weston- super-Mare which must have meant so much to the family.

The inscription, 'To the unfading memory' which was engraved in 1938 would turn out to be true. We have never forgotten Raymond. The tragedy of his death has been passed on to me. I would have loved to know him.

Gloria Elizabeth Lloyd born 26 December 1926. Died in an air crash with her family in Rijeka (former Yugoslavia) on 21 May 1971. They were buried at St. Giles' Church, Ickenham. Married to Derek Orchard. Children: Jacqueline, Michael and Antony, were aged 12, 9 and 7 when they died in the air crash. They lived in Ickenham (Middlesex) at 18 Ivy House Road.

APPENDIX III

HIS SCHOOL
REPORT FROM
CLIFTON COLLEGE
Bristol 1935

CLIFTON COLLEGE.

Name Lloyd, Charles Courtenay House P(J) - N.T.(P.) N.T.

Born 1st May 1919 Entered May 1928 Left April 1935

Previous School Avondale, 20 College Road, Clifton

DREAMY, GOOD AT LATIN BUT WEAK AT MATHS AND SCIENCE, UNABLE
TO EXPRESS HIS FEELINGS. 'HE LEFT TOO YOUNG FOR ONE TO BE ABLE TO
JUDGE WHETHER HE WOULD DEVELOP ANY LEADERSHIP BUT THERE ARE
SIGNS THAT HE MIGHT DO SO.' 'A PERFECTLY RELIABLE BOY'.

217

APPENDIX IV

CELEBRATIONS FOR COURTENAY LLOYD'S HUNDREDTH BIRTHDAY

1 May 2019

CELEBRATIONS FOR COURTENAY LLOYD'S
HUNDREDTH BIRTHDAY 1 May 2019

For this milestone birthday there were many surprises for Courtenay Lloyd. Other than receiving a card from the Queen he had no idea of any of them and was just expecting a cake, a family lunch, a birthday card and a present. But he got so much more. After all, not many people reach the age of a hundred so he deserved a full blown celebration to bring a twinkle to his eyes and make an old man happy on that day.

I am so pleased to know that you are celebrating your one hundredth birthday on 1st May, 2019. I send my congratulations and best wishes to you on such a special occasion.

Elizabeth R

Mr. Courtenay Lloyd

CARD FROM THE QUEEN.

RECOGNITION FROM THE KING OF NORWAY

I had written to the King of Norway (see Appendix V) to ask him to send greetings and give recognition to an old British Navy officer who had contributed to the liberation of his country and who had been awarded the Freedom Medal from his grandfather, King Haakon. He responded affirmatively. I was amazed to receive an email from the King's private secretary on behalf of the king himself. The card arrived in February 2019 and was kept hidden until Courtenay's big day. So there was a card from a Queen and a card from a King that day!

RECOGNITION FROM CLIFTON COLLEGE BRISTOL - HIS SCHOOL FROM 1928 - 1935

His old school responded warmly to my letter to headmaster Dr. Tim Greene informing them of my father's upcoming hundredth birthday. Apart from sending him a card and planning an article in the school magazine to come out later in the year, they also honoured him with a very special tribute. They decided to raise the OC (old Cliftonian) flag from the Wilson Tower on 1 May 2019 with the promise of a video to follow as, of course, he couldn't be there to see it. For it to have been flown on my father's hundredth birthday is the biggest honour the school could bestow on him. The pupils at the school also sang happy birthday to my father from the chapel and later sent a video.

RECOGNITION FROM SELWYN COLLEGE CAMBRIDGE WHERE HE STUDIED MODERN LANGUAGES

I had been in touch with the Roger Mosey, Master of his alma mater Selwyn College, who just happens to have been an old pupil of Bradford Grammar School during my father's time there. He is perhaps more famous for his illustrious career with the BBC. According to college records Courtenay Lloyd is the oldest living Selwynite, something very special for the college to celebrate. They too honoured this milestone birthday with a card and an article in the college magazine. They even sent a member of staff to come out and interview him for the article. Erin Bond, the development manager for Selwyn College, visited him on 8 April 2019 which was a great tribute to him from his old college.

BRADFORD GRAMMAR SCHOOL (BGS) WHERE HE TAUGHT MODERN LANGUAGES, FRENCH, GERMAN AND RUSSIAN AND OCCASIONALLY SWEDISH AND NORWEGIAN FROM 1964 - 1983

BGS also sent a card from the headmaster and informed me of their plans to include an article in The Bradfordian, the school magazine. Lindsey Davis, development director, and her team also reached out to old boys from my father's era to tell them of his upcoming birthday and my father was inundated with cards from all over the world from people who have known him during his fascinating life.

ROYAL NAVY ASSOCIATION

The Royal Navy also responded warmly and sent greetings to Courtenay as former Lt. C. Lloyd of the RNVR in WWII. He was very happy to get a card from his beloved navy.

THE BIOGRAPHY

This biography of course was presented to him as a birthday present on 1 May 2019

THE LLOYD FAMILY TREE

Andrew Dale prepared The Lloyd Family Tree with my help as a gift to Courtenay Lloyd. The tree was built on the Ancestry.com site and presented in the form of a beautiful hard back book with information on many of his ancestors. The tree itself was made into a framed poster and spans six generations, from his great-great grandfather to his grandchildren.

PARTY ON THE DAY

At home, there was a small party with all his favourite food followed by a massive cake with lots of whipped cream, all the many presents and cards, as well as the warmth and love of his family. Guests included his niece Zuka, Amanda Leonard-Myers and Andrew Dale, who came out especially from England and France.

BIRTHDAY PRESENTS

He received many but perhaps the most significant for him was an original copy of *The Times* published on 1 May 1919, I think it was this book that my father appreciated most of all. I handed it to him saying "you have read many books in your life but you have never read a book about yourself". He couldn't believe it and read it three times in a row and it is still on his desk today. I asked him whether I had many any mistakes and he said no. I am so happy I was able to publish this book during his lifetime. Writing it with input from him also brought me much closer to my beloved father and for me this book is one of the most important projects in my life.the day of his birth. He also very much appreciated the great big hamper of chocolates that included his favourites: Turkish Delight, Aero mint chocolate, Walnut Whips, Bounty Bars, Milky Ways, and even Snow Balls, as well as Polo mints.

APPENDIX V

LETTER TO THE KING OF NORWAY AND THE CARD HE SENT TO MY FATHER FOR HIS HUNDREDTH BIRTHDAY ON 1 MAY 2019

LETTER TO THE KING OF NORWAY
AND THE CARD HE SENT TO MY FATHER
FOR HIS HUNDREDTH BIRTHDAY ON
1 May 2019

To His Majesty King Harald V   From Mrs. M. Lloyd
The Royal Court   C/Guadalquivir 35
The Royal Palace   Villaviciosa de Odón
P.O. Box 1 Vika   Madrid 28670
0010 Oslo, Norway   Spain.

Madrid 4th December, 2018.

Subject: The 100th birthday of veteran Royal Navy officer, Lt. Charles Courtenay Lloyd (b. Tamworth, UK 1st May 1919) who contributed to the Liberation of Norway in WW2.

Your Majesty, King Harald V.

This is the first time I have ever written to a king and I do not know the protocol, so please excuse me for that. I do not know either whether your eyes will ever see this letter but I will give it a try. The matter in hand is important to me and to an old British Naval officer who contributed to the Liberation of Norway in WW2, my Father, Charles Courtenay Lloyd who lives with me, his only daughter, in Spain. I did not know who to reach out to, so thought the higher I go, the more likely this matter will get the attention it deserves from Norway. And you can't go higher than a king.

You see, my Father, who knows nothing of this letter, will be 100 on 1st May 2019 and I am planning for his celebrations now. I will of course be in touch with Buckingham Palace for the traditional 100th birthday card from the Queen of England but have read he may not qualify for it as he no longer lives in England, his country of birth.

However, Norway means an awful lot to him, more than I can explain in this letter. Your Grandfather, King Haakan VII awarded him the "Frihetsmedalje" for "outstanding services in connection with the liberation of Norway". I'm afraid that when he moved to Spain 13 years ago, the medal got lost but I do have a clipping from a newspaper to prove it, a copy of which I am embedding at the end of this letter. I wonder whether your war records may include his medal. It's such a pity it got lost.

Once Norway was liberated, my Father spent a whole year there helping the country back on its feet. That is where he learned to love your country and when he learned the language. In fact, when he resumed his degree in Modern Languages at Selwyn College, Cambridge University, after the War, he majored in German and Scandinavian languages, Norwegian being his favourite. Not many English people speak Norwegian and he must be the only English centenarian to do so. That itself deserves recognition I think. He still reads in Norwegian today. I once witnessed a Norwegian citizen speak to him in your language, who told me that my Father spoke it like a native. When he finds it difficult to sleep at night, still today, at the age of 99, with his amazing memory, he does so by naming rivers and lakes in Norway from A to Z! He has been back many times and one of his last solo trips was to Oslo when he was about 94!

He went on to be a very successful teacher of languages at a prestigious school in England (Bradford Grammar School) where old pupils still remember him teaching them Russian, French, German and even Norwegian to some of them - the latter in his lunch hour. He left a lasting impression on many of them.

So what do I want from the King of Norway you may ask? Well, something very simple for you; a personal 100th birthday greeting in the form of a letter or card addressed to him and in recognition of his war efforts and love of Norway. If you write to him in Norwegian he will understand perfectly, although I won't. I can only imagine that there are very few veterans still alive today from the Royal Navy (RNVR then) who contributed to the liberation of Norway in WW2. He may be one of the last and I thought it would important for you to know that. Birthday tidings for such a milestone, his 100th birthday, of which he is well aware and quite excited about, not only from his beloved country Norway but from its King, would certainly bring a sparkle to his eyes and make his day.

I really hope you can fulfil my wish and make an old WW2 veteran and lover of Norway who is actually a very modest man, happy on his 100th birthday next May 1st.

I look forward to your reply,

Yours sincerely,

Masha (Maria) Lloyd

I was amazed when the Royal Palace of Norway responded affirmatively and sent a card from the King, the grandson of King Haakon VII who had awarded my father with the Liberty Medal for his part in the Liberation of Norway. So my father got a card from both a Queen and a King for his hundredth!

HERR CHARLES COURTENAY LLOYD

MINE HJERTELIGSTE GRATULASJONER
I ANLEDNING DERES 100-ÅRS FØDSELSDAG

Harald R

WRITTEN IN NORWEGIAN IT MEANS, HEARTY CONGRATULATIONS ON THE
OCCASION OF YOUR HUNDREDTH BIRTHDAY. SIGNED HARALD R.

APPENDIX VI

COURTENAY THROUGH THE EYES OF HIS PUPILS

QUOTES FROM 'OLD BOYS'

Simon Hewitt, past pupil and compiler of the now famous *Clarence Quotes*, summarized his teacher saying:

'I think we all found your father a very nice man - a man of integrity, and an idealist. I think these were his most impressive qualities (and am sure still are). His very occasional outbursts of anger were always short-lived and invariably deserved. He is one of the funniest men I have ever come across, not always intentionally so, but I suspect more often than one might have surmised. In the classroom he was a tremendous showman - perhaps a form of escapism, given that your mother seems to have ruled the roost at home. He was a very strong teacher with an indomitable sense of purpose.'

Below are just a few extracts from their many emails and messages with their feelings and memories - they are too numerous to reproduce here in their entirety.

DAVID WHITLAM (EX-HEAD BOY) 1976 - 1978

'Masha, I got your blog from Michael Forte, a recently reacquired BGS friend. Your dad taught me Russian in 1976-78 and he sent me to Tony Stokes at Univ Oxford. I subsequently lived in St Petersburg. Your dad was the greatest influence on my entire academic life and I'd be grateful if you could tell him a huge 'привет' (hello) from Whitlam, whom he referred to as 'the phenomenon', which resulted in much teasing, I can tell you!!'

David Whitlam also told me my father had taught him Norwegian when he was in 4X aged 12, and later, Swedish O level which was not part of the school curriculum, something he did in his lunch hour and something I never knew about.

JON STARKEY REFERRING TO DAVID WHITLAM'S COMMENT.

'David excelled at everything at BGS as far as I remember - cross country running, modern languages, and head of school too. It is not a surprise to me, as you know, that many old boys reach out and are absolutely sincere when they say, "Your dad was the greatest influence on my entire academic life."'

JON STARKEY'S OWN MESSAGE - A PUPIL IN THE 1970S AND 80S

'Mr. Lloyd, so many hundreds of boys passed through your classes. In 99% of the cases, you will never know what influence and impact you had on their lives. Here I hope you will see a concrete example of what a difference your teaching could make and I hope it can bring some pleasure and sense of professional satisfaction and pride - be assured that I, like many other former pupils, highly value our days at school with the teaching staff of BGS. I could never have imagined that, thanks to those Russian language skills, I would be presenting in Singapore about the Russian and Central Asian energy insurance markets, or travelling to Iran on behalf of AIG as an "observer" at a conference. The Russian string on my bow opened so many opportunities and sent me all over the world, well beyond the confines of West Yorkshire. Thank you and I will be forever grateful.'

ALSO FROM JON STARKEY

'There are so many of us spread across the globe who owe much to Mr. Lloyd's teaching qualities and inspiration. I could wager that if someone was able to collect the statistical data for A and S levels, the number of A grades, merits and distinctions achieved by his students would be astounding, as would the percentage gaining entry to Oxford, Cambridge and other top universities. We all wish him well'.

JOHN ASQUITH MESSAGE TO MY FATHER (1968 to 1975)

'At school Courtenay - or Clarence as for some reason we all called him - taught me both French and Russian, but it is especially for his enthusiasm and determination as a Russian teacher that I remember him.

He spent hours coaching me outside of school-time to acquire a good accent and delivery for a Russian Speaking Competition (which I won) and many more hours ensuring that I had the necessary grounding to make further study of the language a success.

He also lent me records of Russian operas and choral music and so sparked a lifelong interest in this field. In fact I now work as an opera coach specialising in Russian repertoire as well as being a choral conductor. In recent years I have conducted concerts in Moscow and St Petersburg, appeared with Russian ensembles here in the UK, and on one occasion stood in for a soloist at the State Glinka Capella in St Petersburg to perform Rimsky Korsakov's "Song of the Varangian Guest" - first heard on one of your father's records back in about 1974.

I am lucky to have an interesting and rewarding career that has taken me to many different countries, and owe much of the success I have had to Courtenay's teaching'.

SIMON HEWITT

'Our Russian teacher was Mr C.C. Lloyd known, presumably because it began with a C, as Clarence. He had never previously taught me, though I had occasionally passed him in the corridor. With his deep-set eyes, and Bobby Charlton-coiffed strands of grey hair, he looked frowningly austere, quasi-sepulchral.

Our class was homely. There were only eight or nine of us. Up close he was different. His eyes were a pale, piercing blue, and he liked to laugh. During lessons we laughed a great deal. Sometimes, I regret to say, we laughed about Clarence, and his crumpled suit, and his chalk-covered gown, and his ceaselessly errant chalk (which sometimes, though surprisingly rarely, we had hidden)". Clarence had panache all right, and charisma, and a brain as big as a bullock. A palpably good man, with the naïvety and wisdom of a holy fool. But more often we laughed with him about the quirks of Soviet life. 'This'll put a crack in the proud Soviet boast about inflation' he chuckled one morning, thumbing through a three-week-old copy of Pravda. 'Taxi fares are going up!'

JAMES CROOKES

'You were indeed one of the teachers who inspired me most at school and, in particular, the person who inspired my interest in languages. You taught me French for two years, in the 4th form and Transitus, where you were my form master, and I remember presenting you with an engraved pen on behalf of the class when you retired at the end of that year. Another memory, or collection of memories, is of sitting next to you every lunchtime when the whole class sat on one long table, and we would dole out the food. It was during those lunchtimes that you would tell us about many of your experiences, your love for languages and travel, and something of your time at Cambridge and the intervening war. I remember you telling us that, when you retired, we would be able to find you down at Bradford Central Library, writing down vocabulary and learning new languages - it was clearly such a passion for you! In fact, as my mother will recall, I was very keen to start learning Russian in the sixth form as a result, but she would not let me, as I had so much music practice to do that she felt I would not cope with 4 A levels!

At that time, I was considering reading Music at University, but in fact I changed my mind and chose to study Languages. I went to King's College Cambridge, where I read Modern & Medieval Languages (French, German and Linguistics, with a real focus on philosophy, history of French and the Teutonic languages, and historical linguistics) which gave me the chance to live in Paris for a year. You were a true inspiration to me at school, Mr. Lloyd, and the love of languages and real work ethic that you instilled have opened so many doors for me. I can only hope that my children have the privilege of being taught by someone like you at BGS, who expands their horizons, opens up opportunities for them, and enables them to look back on school with happiness'.

MICHAEL BLACKBURN FORTE 1969 - 1976 BUSINESS STRATEGIST FOR BT

'I remember when I was doing my Russian A-level, Mr Lloyd forcibly impressed on me the need to learn more vocabulary and made me promise, "scout's honour", that I would do so! Well, I wasn't a scout (which he knew!), but I must have taken notice of him, because

I managed to get an A grade in my A-level and subsequently an Open Scholarship to Hertford College, Oxford! From the age of 12 when I first encountered your father as my form master in 4X to the age of 19 when I left BGS he was the formative influence in developing my love of languages and I have very fond memories of him. I wish you all the best with the biography and I wish him all the best too as he approaches his amazing 100 years. Michael'.

ANDY MYERS 1966 - 1972 FINANCE DIRECTOR

'My memories of Courtenay at school were of being slightly intimidated on my first day or so in his form. He seemed quite serious and strict in comparison with the more outwardly gregarious Len Butler who was my first form master on entering BGS.

This impression soon passed however and I realised quickly that he was both a kindly and patently learned man, who seemed to me to have endless patience with even the most errant members of his class. However I also recall him losing his temper a couple of times when pushed to extremes. Such occurrences provoked "shock and awe" in the class almost on a par with one's quiet local vicar suddenly using the 'F' word in church.

These rare outbursts were something I was later to observe occasionally at his home when one of his own offspring ventured beyond the tolerance zone.

The late sixties and early seventies were times when, for most of us anyway, teachers were still revered as serious authority figures both by pupils and their parents.

In the early seventies I became one of the gang enjoying Masha and her brother's parties at the Lloyd household in Heaton Grove, where to my amazement Courtenay and Elena would remain in residence, albeit out of sight. But not because (if this happened in more recent times) they were trying to be cool parents and be their kids 'mates', but simply because they were non-judgmental and accepted young people as adults, and were for the most part genuinely unphased by the antics of a bunch of teenagers pushing the boundaries. My own parents would have had an apoplectic fit and asked everyone to leave if I'd attempted to host a similar event in my home. In truth I would have begged them not to be in the house! The Lloyds always made me feel more like an undergraduate when chatting with them not a fifth or sixth former.

Yet despite their laid back and accepting attitude my own upbringing made me slightly uncomfortable on such occasions being a pupil in a teacher's home, and to this day I have never been able to address Courtenay as anything other than Mr. Lloyd. It just wouldn't seem appropriate and is a mark of real respect from my standpoint.

I was thrilled to meet up again with Courtenay many years later when Amanda (Masha's 'oldest' friend) and I re-met and married in 2005 and to our great pleasure he was able to come over from Spain to attend our wedding in Surrey and giving us Chairman Mao's biography as a wedding present. Subsequently whenever we have visited Masha and Eladio in Spain, Courtenay would gobble up news I brought of former pupils and occasionally staff. His eyes would immediately twinkle with that mischievous "Clarence" smile and he would repeat the name of whoever may be the topic of conversation, savouring the laboured and emphasised pronunciation of their name like the first sip of a fine claret. Courtenay was a 'word gourmet' such that when he frequently did it with specific verbs and nouns in class he made you think you had never heard the word before in your life. Get a difficult French pronounciation correct in his class and if lucky you would be awarded a back copy of *Paris Match*. It might not seem like much but it made me feel like I'd been awarded a medal.

One final memory that sums up his kindness and welcoming nature was how he treated a Polish student Adrian Korynek who joined the class half way through the school year, having just arrived with his mother in England. Not least because Mr. Lloyd pronounced his surname properly of course, but because by the end of the year an extremely shy boy who must have felt rather overwhelmed by the school and surrounded by established friendship groups, flourished, became a competent linguist and had made friendships due in no small part to Courtenay encouraging some of us behind the scenes to invite Adrian to our homes for tea or to hang around. If Courtenay hadn't taken it upon himself to do this I am quite sure that Adrian would have continued to feel isolated and like an outsider in the boys' school culture that existed at the time, and where such spontaneous acts of friendship may have been sneered at or seen as some kind of weakness.

I wish Mr. Lloyd a wonderful 100th birthday with his family. Without doubt one of a kind.'

THE CLARENCE QUOTES TITLED 'STALIN'S BREATH'. Compiled by Simon Hewitt while in his lessons with my father:

RUSSIANS

Russians know everything. And they're subtle!

Russians are so motivated and efficient!

My God, if you travelled on the Trans-Siberian Railway they'd soon know all about your great-grandfather.

It's easy to say all this from this chair. In Russia they'd say "My God! I've got a different point of view!" That's what makes Russians such terribly interesting people.

My God! That's strong language ! They speak through their teeth, you know, muttering oaths. They're expressive - AND SUBTLE!

You must develop Soviet earnestfulness!

Russians don't have wishy-washy ideas about treating children as delicate things. They give 'em a few good bashings!

Desks are a very important part of Soviet life.

There's a lack of snobbery about Russians that's rather attractive. Russian doctors are more humane.

In Russia you get cigarettes called Friendship or Polar Dog.

They grow their own cigarettes. All right, joke over! I mean tobacco. It's scented. Soviets smoke like mad. They smoke like chimneys. I must confess I rather like Soviet cigarettes.

Russians have a yen for culture. Yen, yearning.

Russian churches smell of incense and are not garishly lit.

You can read through the lines in Soviet newspapers - all kinds of titbits about rude bus-conductors.

Bells have a sentimental streak in them. Russians play sentimental songs to Russians living in America hoping all the émigrés will rush to the nearest Soviet consulate and sign up to go back to Russia.

This'll put a crack in the proud Soviet boast about inflation - taxi fares are going up.

The Russians are a great people for gestures !

So what we'll have to do, comrades, is be like the Soviets, and drink very weak tea with lemon. Tea is a luxury drink. Four or five teabags should last you all week!

Good old English teeth-rotting white bread! It's disgusting, really. BROWN bread's good for you.

Every whim can be satisfied if you've got the money. Not so in Eastern Europe! The state of the nation's teeth is better in Iron Curtain countries.

Russians can seem terribly stodgy people. They're not really.

Kremlinologists sift through boring Pravda and Izvestya to see who'll be next Prime Minister. And high-placed Czech generals give us lots of information!

In Russia, alcoholism is a national disease - make no mistake!

You don't get way-out pop groups in the USSR. They're musically much more literate.

Don't forget your Caucasian Capers and Russian Romances.

I've just read this soppy book about a Russian aristocrat on holiday in Siberia. He meets a local girl, etc. etc.

You reckon you're "cultured" in inverted commas if you read Reveille or something. YOU OUGHT TO BE SHOT! They don't go in for rubbishy tripe like that in the Soviet Union. They'd all read the Financial Times.

Borzois are very elegant, graceful Russian dogs, with long heads and small muzzles. I think so, anyway. I don't know anything about them, really. If you do Russian A-level, I've got a huge long prose for you about Russian borzois.

Read Russian history books - "feudal this", "feudal that"....

Wedding-cake style of architecture - aesthetical people think it's horrid. It strikes me as being not unattractive.

Steam trains are very attractive: Russians use birch logs for fuel. They smell nice. Next time you're in Istanbul take a trip along the Persian border.

The Ice Maiden is a Russian heroine, only she melts in Spring.

Who's heard of people doing Russian theses on the Toy Industry? Well, that's dead right! Russians want hard cash !

Peter the Great died in the early 1720s. Today he'd probably have been Archbishop of Canterbury, because he built this colossal monastery. Well, not that big. Called the New Maiden. Yes. About half-an-hour from the centre of Moscow. Well, 20 minutes if you go by Metro. People are impressed by its AUSTERE MONUMENTALITY and SEVERE SIMPLICITY.

Lo and behold! It's a crackly speech by Lenin.

Trotsky is still an anathema. He was a good, hardworking, solid, excellent chap.

You've all heard of Molotov cocktails? Molotov was a stone-faced, hard-line Stalinist if ever there was one! He also had various tame names.

Towards the end of this street in Leningrad, which is one or two miles long, perhaps three, a couple of miles anyway, well let's say it's a few miles long. Well, you go through pages and pages of Russian literature and music on a tram. You get the conductor announcing over the intercom "This is Leo Tolstoy Street." Intercom is superb!

Read Russian poetry! Pushkin is so laconic.

Peter Pan's probably been translated into Russian. Winnie-the-Pooh CERTAINLY has.

Russians are phenomenal. But we British have got some good points ourselves.

VOCABULARY

Did you sleep good, bad or indifferent? Well, to wake you up, let's REAP THROUGH that vocab!

We learn chunks every so often - chunks of vocab every night. They're entirely and utterly relevant.

Let's take a REAL SEARING LOOK at this sheet of vocab.

Okay? Any difficulties? No! Good. Well, let's have a real injection of vocab. I've heard that word used by the Berlitz School, so let's really drill it in.

Hello! That's a good word to remember! A lot of Biblical words are trinkling into Russian.

Ham, the son of Noah, is the Russian for Cad.

"Mad" - having gone down from the mind.

Smoke is "dim", you see. That's a very nice little synonym for you.

The "West" means falling behind. Yes, falling behind. That's right! And "wind" means weather. These words are called calques.

Russians do a lot of swearing, damning and dashing. It's their verb to give.

It's Russian for Tall Weed. Put it down!

As time goes on, here's a word you ought to know. We all ought to know it, really. It means a house on an island in a Russian lake.

"On your face not." You're looking awful! My God, you look dreadful!

You know this word "nuance"? Good Russian word. That's why it's French.

I know it's a hellish word, but there is something about the Russian for "wolfish" that we cannot seem to grab. We'll have to plug away.

Let's say it with courage, determination and conviction: read, mark, learn and inwardly digest, as the old Biblical prayer goes.

This is a word I've been ABSOLUTELY DYING for us to use for months, but we haven't had it officially. It means Village.

An agronomist is someone who goes and tells farmers all about piggeries and things.

There's a word for "little shop" which I'm told is peasanty and going out of fashion. Archaic, you might say - obsolescent.

It's not a river - it's a snakey lake.

Pushkin was a man of guns!

I shall probably be giving you Tchaikovsky Street. You know, some Serbo-Croat football players are sometimes called Tchaikovsky. Mr Seagull!

Let's copy these words down, every single one of them!! Write it down… PLEASE write it down! Yes, another one for goodness' sake!!

It's a famous poem by Pushkin. Out-of-the-way words come in left right and centre.

From Sanskrit, probably. I'll look it up in my Russo-Sanskrit etymological dictionary. It tells me everything.

"Many vodkas" - yes! Sounds plausible. But you should have a copy of this etymological dictionary.

Hands up if you're interested in etymology!

I'll get my big super etymological dictionary RIGHT NOW. Where's it gone? Oh, here it is. This real gem of the dictionary is produced by the Academy of Science. Yes: 21 volumes! Ah yes, now, er, let's see, right…. what am I looking up? I've forgotten.

This word farrago. What does it mean? Fiasco? Harum-scarum? Latin for hotch-potch, it says here. So there we are.

A lovely word, except it's terribly temperamental and unpredictable.

It means stodgy, dry, dull, buttoned-up, unemotional and boring.

How many s's in compass? Sorry? Three!! Good Lord! Are you sure? Well yes, I suppose so. I just forget how to spell these words now and again.

Ballet in Russian has one l. You get confused after a while.

A "friend" - you have a polarization of interests. Well, not "polarization." Common interests, you might say? Very much so!

Fibberty-gibbet is my type of word. It's got panache, that's the great thing !

GRAMMAR

Put in a nice big fat comma!

Commas are needed by law, even if we're doing it in a jokey way.

"E" with two dots over it. Don't forget the dots!

No dots in the singular, but dots throughout the plural. They're a bit stingy with little dots, you know. But nice big fat commas are essential!

NO two dots, because the STRESS HAS SW-IT-CHED.

Called Mr Flea - two dots!!

The two dots disappear in the oblique cases. Oh my goodness. I've been rather lax! Commas are obligatory!

Here's a little bit of happy news for you. The accusative, genitive, dative and locative singular of feminine nouns ending in a sibilant have the same ending. Well, not always. Some of them do. I can't give you a hard-and-fast rule, I'm afraid.

It won't be yeh because there's no sibilant around.

You'd think it was yeh: but it's HIGHLY IR-REG-U-LAR!

If you're going to get tattooed, put "animate and motion" to remind yourself. And don't omit your sibilants !

YEH! There's been some EH's going around. That's wrong pronunciation, got that? Quite wrong. Okay. Let's all say YEH together, ten times.

You're pronouncing it like German - like Universität. Cut it out! Let's have it yet, for Pete's sake!

MATCH and DOTCH are the only ones that add the YEH. It's mainly because of their sibilants.

"Consonant clusters" - a nice linguistic expression. It's not syntactical, idiomatic or elliptical.

I'm not a champagne expert. It ends in O, so it must be neuter.

Sometimes you can use it adjectivally, but it's much better pre-di-ca-tive-ly.

French "r's" are throaty, English has them near the front of the mouth, but in Russian they're trilled - "Rrr-rrr-rrrr-rrrrr-rrrr!"

Good Lord! Don't forget the animates!

It's masculine, unless you're a girl. Then it's different.

Repeat all that, please, in your most musical voice!

It's quite a meaty week as far as grammar goes, I guess.

Right, now here you have an interesting verb. You've met it for years in Latin and Greek. Got it? TREASURE IT! It's an unavoidable necessity. Hold it! Stop! Not unavoidable. Well, it is really.

Any queries or difficulties? The subject goes dative. The object goes nominative. Is that quite clear ?

Coffee is very unusual. It's masculine.

Trains ROAR into stations? Oh, DRAW into stations. Yes. Trains walk, anyway.

If it's concrete, it's accusative. Yes sir! But let's put it in the genitive!

It's used ONLY IN THE SINGULAR! Well, generally, anyway.

It's highly irregular. Really irreg. It's VERY IRREGULAR so let's get it copied down!

And oh dear oh dear oh dear! Lo and behold, there were some glaz-i's. Glaz-A! Come on, ten times now !

I've got a little play about the Russian genitive plural of "poker."

Tie a knot in your moustache! Avoid sending words meaning "under" to the end.

The things is to be fluent fluent fluent fluent! Snappy answers! Really bark them out!

Let's get on - i.e. let's travel further. Say these long words with a determined sticking-out jaw.

That's a howler ! Sibilants must go yeh! Where's my chalk?

SCHOOL

Where's my chalk ? Oh, it's on top of the blackboard; thank you. Where? What - it was a crack in the wall you say? But where's my chalk? Who's got it? It'll be my form! STUPID OAFS! I'LL THRASH THEM!

I'm frightened of putting up nice Russian posters about Dickens because my form are a set of vandals. Well, not really vandals, you know. They just slob in and chuck ink about.

It's a useful conversational ploy, but I shan't write it on the board this time because I get so covered in chalk.

We'll just have to soldier on. We must hold out, stick it out, and finish the book. That's the great thing.

Nasty little enemies of Russian like wretched school exams. Everything mitigates against it. Next we will consider work for the holidays.

We carry sort of three weeks holiday at this school, which is terribly bad for Russian.

You get people who'll do well in the term, fairly conscientious, get good marks in your exams, take home your good report.... But they aren't your genuine modern linguist! They aren't curious!! They won't do things off their own bat!!!

I've just read in a self-satisfied report by a member of the 8th Glamorgan Education Committee that British Education is the best in the world. ABSOLUTE TRIPE! And I'm not talking about the higher echelons, either.

It's just a rubber-stamp organization with a wad of fivers for all concerned.

I've got some bits of calendar for you! Here's the times of the, er, of when the moon rises and sets... Here's a dum-dum one about how to make a frock or something.

Here's a piece of calendar for you - a picture of a girl. She's a shop-worker. A rather fetching girl in a steel helmet. Here's a rather stodgy headline for you. All headlines have pictures of steel-helmeted shop-workers.

"The bureaucracy and its misdemeanours" it says on this bit of calendar. Doesn't mean anything much.

Karl Marx was the FOUNDER of Communism! He was the brains behind the scheme! Russians memorize his date of birth.

Karl Marx died on 14 March 1883! Well, that's what it says here, on this bit of calendar.

Here's a bit of calendar for you. How to make yourself a parachute. No, I'll keep it myself. Have this instead... something about hares jumping.

Picture dictionaries have cats jumping off tables.

"Approach". You go up and under. Pod. In your picture-dictionary you'll find some very good pictures of dogs hiding under boxes.

Yes! Learn everything - that's right! The whole shebang!

GEOGRAPHY

Read Intourist Magazine! It's vibrant!

I've got a German atlas at home. It's the biggest atlas you've ever seen. I can scarcely carry it around. I got it from a German prisoner-of-war. It's got the German names for towns in Czechoslovakia. I've spent hours pleasantly thumbing through it.

Roadlessness - i.e. without a road. Mother Russia has plenty of peasanty roads.

The Trans-Siberian Railway is like the Trans-Alaska Highway.

Europe begins at the end, in the Urals.

Gorky's just east of Moscow. Well, about 400 miles away.

This envelope has a Soviet stamp. It's from Minsk - 53, Worm Street.

Lithuanians hate Russians. They're ardent Catholics, you know. They hate their guts! They just hate them! THE HATRED IS THERE!

Have a minute's rest. It's a big town in the Urals.

When I'm free, I don't spend the evening watching tripe. My God no! I twiddle the knobs on my £14 wireless-set getting short-wave Hungarian radio. It's music, you know! Not like Radio Luxembourg! Pop music is music for the illiterate.

I'll tell you one thing as well: if you want to get hold of a fortune, buy a 1914 Baedeker's guide to Russia.

We're right next door to the Soviet Union! Well, we're not really. Poland's nearer.

Poles coming to West Germany are dazzled by the surfeit of onions, week-in week-out. They just can't understand it.

Steppes are like prairies. Bullets whistle through the air.

Vladivostok is the Power Of The East.

The Urals are sparkling with metals.

They really do bark, the Germans!

Haven't you heard of Radio Liberty? It could be said to have been a cradle of Prussian militarism. Well no, it couldn't. Sorry.

The Fall of Berlin is a magnificent Soviet colour film of the mid-50s. Well, probably early '50s. It's got lots of pictures of a pipe-smoking Stalin plucking rose-trees in the Kremlin.

When we were in Moscow, we saw this Russian film. Well, it was a Polish film that had been dubbed.

It's a scandal that we don't have our radio weather-forecasts read with poetry! They're so deadpan... it's an absolute disgrace! But there's poetry about the shipping forecast. I enjoy that. I'd love to receive world temperatures from the Met Office through the post.

Switch on your short-wave radio. You've got Arabic right on a plate!

Teach yourself Maltese!

French, Cubans and Congolese all speak the same language, namely Russian.

Just look at a map of the world! Half of Europe speaks Russian! Russian opens up Yugoslavia and Bulgaria! And Russian is the key to Comparative Philology and Etymology!

SAYINGS

Silence Is Golden, Talking Is Silver. That's an old Russian saying.

Here's a good little proverb for you: Don't sit with your arms folded, don't see boredom.

There's a funny Russian expression. It doesn't mean anything really. Laziness was born before us.

Krushchov was always coming out with peasanty expressions.

Lo and behold! It's on page, page, er eight, no, page three, I think. Yes it is! So, as they say, Bob's Your Uncle or, as in Russia, Everything's In Your Hat.

Say My Aunt Lives In Kiev! Russians are always saying it.

Here's a funny Russian proverb which nobody laughs at: Drink tea and know where the seagulls are flying. Here's another: In Kiev there is an uncle, in Odessa there is an elderberry tree.

Many edges of the forest - an unlikely phrase but very grammatically useful.

If he's kicking over the traces, the form committee hauls him over the coals.

Ah! Put down this nice expression: Ideological Disputes Over Communist Jargon.

Russians have a little saying: To know someone, you've got to a eat a pound of salt with them.

Rabies - ah yes ! What's known as Siberian Ulcer.

Here's a pithy little expression: Pseudo-Communists are Radishes. Yes - red on the outside, white on the inside.

Here's a silly one! Russians call people white as soot.

As they say in Russia - speed is only good in the catching of fleas.

All Power to the Soviets! You've all heard it - it's a mighty good slogan.

Russian factory-workers all shout We shall export or die!

I'm interested in the Russian phrase for mumps. It means little pigs in your mouth.

Doggish cold - that's a good expression. Put it down!

In the Russian army the hectic hour after manoeuvres is called the Dead Dog hour.

There's a famous Russian story called The Tale of the Sturdy Turnip.

Russians think Europeans are pigeons.

You'd call even an old codger a "young man" in the Soviet Union!

If Russians like you, they tell you you're a shop-worker.

Together in war. Together in peace. Together in work. Yes! Like a collective farm.

Eau de Cologne used to be called Stalin's Breath in Russia.

It's a dog's life all right these days.

I used to live in Bristol. I look back at it with affection. It's got a certain dignity. Bradford is inward-looking.

If I had my time over again I'd teach English abroad. No, not in Saudi Arabia. Somewhere like Morocco.

It's a little bit of a piggery - a swine. A damn nuisance!

Their foul language is pretty foul.

Uhum. Aha. Uhurm. Yes. Uhum. Go on. *Ssshh!*

I WANT PEACE! I'm not a way-out Leftist.

People campaign for dissidents outside St George's Hall. Leeds Jews picket Soviet choirs. Go to Pickard's Garage in Huddersfield for your Soviet entertainment.

My record's all scratched. The acoustics in here are appalling.

Pepsi Cola refreshes your soul! - It's terrible. Stilted, stodgy... Oh, I've used that word again!

There is another side to Russian - well, 'Chinese' it says here. For 'Chinese' read 'Russian' - it's the same thing. Or Japanese. If you used Mandarin Chinese at a Frizinghall takeaway they wouldn't understand you.

A man came up to me in the street. It was in London. No it wasn't - I mean Dover. He was a Romanian. We got talking. It turned out that he was Bulgarian. He asked me why all English people didn't speak German.

Ed Stewart? Rod Stewart?? Who's he? From Melody Maker, I suppose!

... a much larger class with some thick people in it. One of them was strumming an electric guitar.

Perfect is a rotten word because, well, it isn't rotten really.

Here's a museum near where boys make joint efforts to consolidate Czech-Soviet anti-Hitlerite friendship.

He's a swine and a saboteur. I used to tell him that.

I'm not a complaining sort.

Ta-ra, cheery bye... one thing I can't stand is people who say 'Bye!' It drives my through the wall! I may be standing on ceremony here, but why can't people say 'Goodbye'? T'reet, see you... it's disgusting! A'll sithee... that's good. I like that.

The 60th most common surname in Lenin before the Revolution was Schmidt. Okay, joke over. I mean Russia.

A holiday in Russia only costs 300 packets of cigarettes.

I've got a thing called 'Key-Facts'. I lend them out for about 20 rubles a time.

I was thinking about this timetable - I went to bed with it. I've got a spare copy of it here. Well, it's not spare really. It's my own.

The Russians are good at ballet because women's calendars have physical jerks on them every other day. Ever seen Russian ballet on the radio?

Be flexible. You've just got to be a terrible gas-bag! Don't worry about your mistakes. Well, you should have nervous breakdown if you make an error!

You've met it in French. Well, not so much French. German certainly.

Who got it wrong? No one? Oh, sorry. Slandering you unnecessarily.

I thought Mrs Rees was your form-master? Oh, your form-mistress.

Let's say it ten times! Well, nine times. It's nearly ten times. There's the bell, thank God.

Are you ill, Fenton?

No.

Glory to God.

A programme I like a lot is Woman's Hour. Ever listen to Woman's Hour, Fenton?

No.

Please remember capital letters at the beginning of a sentence, Fenton. You're a bit wishy-washy.

Old Fenton's getting his x's Greeky.

Wait a minute. Stop! STOP! I was getting tired. That's right, Kiely! Sorry.

Kiely's a peasant. That's right! Well no. Not one of those toiling peasants.

You're a digger, Kiely. You dig the water. When you row you bucket up the water in great big buckets. Well, that's the basic idea.

Kiely lives in Stockholm and he doesn't decline.

Hewitt and Kiely are the future intelligentsia of this country.

I was just going to say you're a genius, Kiely. You look so intellectual, so academic - so perfect. Keep it up!

That's tripe, Kiely.

Are you a Communist, Kiely?

Why 'no', Kiely? Well yes, that's a logical conclusion.

What's a fast cart, Kiely?

Have you written any swinging little poems, Kiely?

You're a good anti-Fascist, probably, Kiely.

Who's the great chess-player in this form? Ah, Bracewell - just the chap.

Bracewell made a few tongue-in-cheek comments about twiddling the knobs on his radio.

The assiduous young man is Bracewell. He is very assiduous.

It's an awfully crude mistake, Adams.

Adams, ask Koskinen if he woke up early on Sunday.

He's a bit queer, but not in that sense.

Keen on Boy Scouts, Adams?

Tell 'em to sit down, Koskinen.

Sit down.

What chapter are we on, Koskinen?

I don't know.

What's Russian for 'live,' Koskinen?

I was just going to ask that.

You're a cad, Koskinen, 'cos you haven't done your homework!

I feel damn insulted! I won't be insulted. I'm hopping mad! I admire Mr Somers for the work he gets out of you. I'm not soft! I shall take a leaf out of Mr Somer's book. I've never known anything like it! From now on it's one hour's extra work or a detention! I won't stand any more!

BIBLIOGRAPHY AND REFERENCES

Secret Classrooms: An Untold Story of the Cold War by Geoffrey Elliott and Harold Shukman. Printed by St. Ermin's Press Book in Great Britain in 2002

In the Mind's Eye: The Memoirs of Dame Elizabeth Hill. Edited by Jean Stafford Smith. Printed in Great Britain by The Book Guild Ltd. 1999

New College School, Oxford: A history, by Matthew Jenkinson

Gotha Almanach: http://www.angelfire.com/realm/gotha/gotha/lieven.html. This is the official registry of European nobility.

HMS *Wells* - http://www.naval-history.net/xGM-Chrono-11US-HMS_Wells.htm

HMS *Mansfield* - https://uboat.net/allies/warships/ship/4298.html

Report of the Rijeka Air Crash in 1971 in which Courtenay's sister Gloria and her family died.http://aviation-safety.net/database/record.php?id=19710523-0&fbclid=IwAR3WN4R4vbqfVRW_D1AH829ffPQ92dHKdLoJZtl8dpS-D9zrT9YR6nkFEtc

Blog Holyhead Stories of a Port

Post 5 Jan 2019. John Collins - 82nd Regiment of Foot, 1827 - 1904 by Barry Hillier

https://holyheadstoriesofaport.com/2019/01/05/john-collins-82nd-regiment-of-foot-1827-1904/

Obituary Dame Elizabeth Hill. *The Independent* 6 January 1997: https://www.independent.co.uk/news/obituaries/obituary-professor-dame-elizabeth-hill-1281970.html

General Register Office, Southport UK

Letters to his sister Gloria Orchard née Lloyd during and after WWII.

Photographs from the collection of family photos belonging to Katriona Fox Lloyd

Photographs from the collection of family photos belonging to Angela Benson

The British Library, East India Company Records (IOR)

Welsh Newspapers online - The National Library of Wales

Royal Navy Disclosure Team - Royal Navy Command Portsmouth.

The Chaplain's Museum Archive: https://www.chaplains-museum.co.uk/archive/record-cards/217697-lloyd-jc-01jpg?#prettyPhoto

The Lloyd Lieven family tree: https://www.ancestry.com/family-tree/tree/158654456

ABOUT THE AUTHOR
Masha (Maria) Lloyd

MASHA LLOYD THE AUTHOR.
PIPPA MY SPOILED MINIATURE DACHSHUND
HAD TO GET INTO A PICTURE IN THIS BOOK.
I WOULDN'T HAVE IT ANY OTHER WAY.

If you have read the biography of my father you will understand that I had quite an extraordinary upbringing. I was born in England (Cambridge) and am half English and half Russian and married a Spaniard and live in Spain. That makes me some sort of cultural and international cocktail and I often wonder what nationality I really feel I am. English of course because I was born there but I feel like a citizen of the world. As for my daughters, born in Spain, they have English, Russian and Spanish blood making them an even more explosive cocktail.

My life is a lot less extraordinary unless you count having married an ex-Catholic priest. In a way, I have followed in my parents' footsteps and have a very happy marriage and family with my rock solid husband Eladio, and our adored daughters Suzy and Olivia.

Life has treated me very well. After graduating in Hispanic Studies at Nottingham University in 1980, I met Eladio that summer and I moved to Spain a year later to live with him and have lived in Madrid ever since. He is 12 years older than I am but you wouldn't notice as he never seems to age. We got married in 1983 and since then our life has had its ups and downs but mostly I have been very lucky. On the whole I am very happy with my lot and have no complaints.

My career started with teaching English to Spanish children but it was obvious from early on that I hadn't inherited my parents' skills at teaching so I turned to the corporate world. I started in an administrative and translator role in a dubious Spanish company. My first job was with Defex. When I applied for the job I had no idea the company exported arms but as jobs were scarce I took it. I spent eight years in an exciting but immoral world, at least for me. On the plus side it took me to arms exhibitions in exotic places such as Athens, Kuala Lumpur, Ankara and to visit even more dubious banks in London during the Iran Iraq war. My next job was with Cadbury Schweppes, the drinks part, not the chocolates unfortunately. I found that extremely boring as I have no love of fizzy drinks. It was in 1990 when I entered the telecommunications sector, just as mobile phones were about to take off. It was in this sector I developed my whole career. It hasn't been easy being a woman in a man's world in Spain. However, with much dedication and hard work, I became the head of communications of Motorola, the communications director of Nokia and latterly the communications director of Yoigo, a Swedish owned mobile phone company. Those were great corporate years when I travelled a lot. Working for Finnish and Swedish companies I came to love the Nordic countries, just as my father does. In 2017 Yoigo was bought by another company and most of the management team was made redundant. Thus I found myself about to turn 60 and unemployed. I had to start from the beginning again. This time I followed in my mother's footsteps and, after the girls left home, took lodgers into our huge house which has many spare rooms. I turned to Airbnb and since I started in January 2017, this house, like my parents' house in Bradford, has become an international hub, with guests coming from the four corners of the earth. Many of these guests have become friends. Thankfully Eladio doesn't have to serve them meals like my father.

I also became a freelance communications consultant and now work for various companies on and off and from home. In reality, now I have the perfect work life balance. I am able to spend time with my husband who is retired, with my father, and with the girls when they are here. Thus I have had time to embark on my first book, the story of my father as he enters his hundredth year.

In my free time I love walking with our dogs, Elsa the labrador, Norah the beagle and little Pippa, the apple of my eye, a miniature chocolate dachshund; I also enjoy reading, cooking, and dinners out with my husband and friends. I love travelling too which of course I have inherited from my parents. My family comes first though after which comes my next great passion, my blog.

I am not a complete stranger to writing as I have been writing a blog since 2005. You can follow our lives here: http://mashalloyd.blogspot. com. It is my passion and I write a post every Sunday without exception. My father gets given a hard copy as soon as I publish a new post and is my most loyal reader.

I have enjoyed writing this book so much that I may now embark on the story of my mother who in life always overshadowed my father and has tried to do the same in this book. Her story is even more fascinating…

Masha
Madrid April 2019
You are welcome to write to me via email: masha.lloyd@googlemail.com
And follow me on my blog: http://mashalloyd.blogspot.com

COURTENAY AND HIS DAUGHTER MASHA WITH THE CARDS FROM THE
QUEEN OF ENGLAND AND THE KING OF NORWAY ON HIS
100th BIRTHDAY - MADRID, 1 MAY 2019.

Printed in Great Britain
by Amazon

80131004R00154